SUPPER
AT
RICHARD'S PLACE

SUPPER AT RICHARD'S PLACE

Recipes from the New Southern Table

Richard Jones

PELICAN PUBLISHING COMPANY
Gretna 2005

Copyright © 2005
By Richard Jones
All rights reserved

The word "Pelican" and the depiction of a pelican are trademarks of Pelican Publishing Company, Inc., and are registered in the U.S. Patent and Trademark Office.

Library of Congress Cataloging-in-Publication Data

Jones, Richard, chef.
  Supper at Richard's Place : recipes from the new Southern table / by Richard Jones.
       p. cm.
  ISBN-13: 978-1-58980-299-5 (alk. paper)
  ISBN-10: 1-58980-299-3 (alk. paper)
  1. Cookery, American—Southern style. 2. Richard's Place (Restaurant) I. Title.
  TX715.2.S68J66 2005
  641.5975—dc22
                                            2005005833

Printed in the United States
Published by Pelican Publishing Company, Inc.
1000 Burmaster Street, Gretna, Louisiana 70053

*To my wife and best friend, Rhonda,
who has the remarkable ability to turn my hopes and
dreams into reality.*

Contents

Acknowledgments 9
Introduction 11
Appetizers 17
Soups and Salads 35
Fish and Seafood 47
Poultry, Meats, and Game 77
Side Dishes 101
Sauses, Salsas, Relishes, and Dressings 119
Breads and Biscuits 129
Desserts 139
Index 157

Acknowledgments

Completing this project is truly a dream fulfilled. Above all, I thank God from whom all blessings flow. I know that it is God's grace and guidance that has made everything that I have achieved possible. Thank you, God, I am forever grateful.

Secondly, I would like to acknowledge the following individuals:

My deceased parents Sam and Cora Jones who nurtured me and provided a wealth of experiences that contributed to making me the person that I am today.

My mother-in-law, Mary Wainwright, who is more like a mother to me, always there to listen and offer her unbiased advice and spiritual guidance. My niece, Corrina Wainwright, who sacrificed several weekends helping my wife type my recipes. My siblings: Virginia, Dorothy, Katherine, and Sam, who always offer objective feedback. My brother-in-laws, Charles and Carey, whom I know that I can always turn to for support and who have always interacted with me equally as one of their brothers.

My sidekick, Jeff, who is not only a loyal customer but also an extremely supportive friend. Pamela, Regina, Arnold, and Seda, the constant "Thursday dinner crew" who continue to remind me that all dreams are possible.

My sous chef, Ed Thompson, who has endured many turbulent times throughout the years that he has worked with me yet remains allegiant. Wayne and Shelly, who keep me amused even when they test my patience. The waitstaff, who skillfully keeps the front of the house in order regardless of how hectic times become.

My culinary arts instructors at the New York Institute of Technology who helped to refine my cooking skills.

My customers who have remained loyal and who help to keep me on a positive path.

Linda Konner, who continued to believe in this project and never gave up, even when I was about to throw in the towel. My editor, Nina Kooij, who was very patient and assuring. The publishing management team at Pelican Publishing Company. Thank you all for helping to strengthen me and help to make this dream come true.

Introduction

Writing this cookbook seems to be a divinely ordered opportunity for me to fulfill two aspirations. Primarily, this work is the result of continual requests from customers who frequent Richard's Place and relentlessly ask for the recipes of their favorite selections from the menu at the restaurant. Secondly, this endeavor presents an occasion for me to honor my father, Samuel Jones. As an unsung cook, my father prepared meals in commercial kitchens and hotels throughout the South feeding dignitaries and celebrities such as Butterfly ("Gone With the Wind") McQueen and columnist Walter Winchell.

Unlike so many other professional chefs, who often refer to the women in their lives who inspired their culinary abilities, my father was my greatest influence. I can fondly recall him preparing dishes for our church's anniversary or special events hosted by the Deacon Board. I always looked forward to standing by his side at his restaurant, the Blue Goose, as he prepared those dishes that everyone awaited with great anticipation. My father was also a hunter and a fisher. He always appeared so regal with his 6' 2" frame dapperly donned in hunting attire. While I am truly proud to have an opportunity to present Southern cuisine in a new and healthier style, it is equally exhilarating to produce a work that will honor my father's contribution as well.

The collections of recipes that I developed for this book are deeply rooted in my Southern upbringing. The recipes are also an outgrowth of my experiences as a transplanted resident of New York. Relocating from Augusta, Georgia, to New York City, provided an opening for me to interact with many people from varied and exciting cultures. Living in the Big Apple makes it virtually impossible to be unaffected by the voluminous cooking styles offered within this major city.

New York is a city within which millions of individuals daily exchange fragments of their diverse cultures. These transactions performed by an ever-growing population create constant change and a melding of new dishes. The constantly changing fares resemble the complementary patterns reflected in a kaleidoscope. In keeping with my Southern roots, I included some very distinct dishes that remain as true to their origin as possible. However, it would be disingenuous not to present some recipes with a renewed overlapping of diverse food ways and cultural influences found throughout ethnic cooking in New York.

The ever-evolving cuisine that I am creating in New York is as eclectic as the melange of the Southern menu. My style of cooking is a natural progression of Southern cooking, considering how it is extremely difficult to separate the interwoven cultural influences that exist in Southern cuisine. The matrix of Southern cooking is as deep and complex as the interconnected relationships that existed among Native Americans, Africans who were transported to the South to work the land, and the European settlers. The original fusion cuisine, Southern food covers a broad range of cooking styles, including soul food, Cajun and Creole cuisines, and the refined delicacies of the wealthy Old South.

Therefore, it is no small wonder that my style of cooking, affectionately referred to as New Southern, transforms and updates a wealth of authentic family recipes in keeping with today's palates and dietary concerns. Combining traditional ingredients while substituting others, New Southern cuisine takes the reader beyond the stereotypical entrees and side dishes. I cook food with the same fervor as my father did decades ago, with great reverence for my early childhood experience, encouraging the savoring of exquisite food and straightforward flavors.

I have been very careful to preserve the old-world piquancy and protect this cuisine from changing food trends. However, times do change and as we become more familiar with healthier eating habits, I cannot see why anyone would resist dishes that offer a fullness of flavors while protecting one's health. We have been in business at Richard's Place for over ten years, and I have yet to hear one lasting complaint about New Southern cuisine. Whenever I appear on a variety of cooking shows customers subsequently flock to the restaurant to experience my interpretation of Southern cooking.

It may be virtually impossible for everyone interested in New Southern cuisine to have the opportunity to visit the restaurant. Therefore, my ultimate desire is to encourage those interested in cooking, to recreate the dishes that I prepare for customers who enjoy home-style Southern cooking in a major Northern city. These foolproof recipes have been tested and will empower the home cook to bring guests begging for more.

The recipes that I offer for appetizers prepared with New Southern flair are flavorful and uncomplicated. These starters complete an ideal party buffet, or when served in larger portions and perhaps with soup or a salad, can make a meal.

The next unit presents recipes for soups and salads. My choices of soup recipes reflect the ethnic influences that show up in the New Southern tureen along with down home basic comforts such as old-fashioned vegetable chicken soup. I thoroughly enjoy using a variety of textures and colors when making great salads. These contrasts are equally as important as the ingredients. Therefore, the recipes that I included for salads reflect this philosophy of mine.

With such an abundance of fish and seafood in supermarkets, I strongly encourage cooks to incorporate some of the recipes presented for seafood and fish into their menu planning. Due to the fact that catfish is a very versatile and low-fat fish, I share numerous ways to prepare this healthy catch along with a broad range of recipes in the seafood arena.

I truly want to encourage cooks to prepare traditional Southern dishes in a healthier way. I demonstrate this approach to cooking throughout the book. The section devoted to poultry, meats, and game definitely presents new twists on traditional methods of cooking these food items.

My recipes for side dishes will delight most vegetarians and are excellent when paired appropriately with poultry, meat, and fish recipes. When eating at many "traditional" southern tables, I have had too many experiences where the cook has overcooked the vegetables. In a desperate effort to remedy this method of cooking, I also share tips for preparing vegetables.

I love sauces. Although sauces will not save overcooked dishes, they definitely will enhance well-prepared meals. I have included a wide variety of recipes for sauces, relishes, and gravies that will tempt guests to lick their plates.

Any Southerner knows that breads and biscuits are a staple of good, homemade Southern cooking. Even with the dieting trend that currently encourages diners to refrain from eating carbohydrates, I believe that it is possible to eat most foods in moderation. Therefore, I have created recipes with hopes of giving any cook a chance to recapture the comforting tastes and smells of homemade breads and biscuits.

Lastly, I cannot think of a better way to end a scrumptious meal than with a wonderful dessert. In keeping with the overall theme of this book, I have given a range of recipes for desserts that are easy to prepare and will have guests thinking hours went into preparing these delicious treats.

It will be hard not to get an oversized ego when guests begin to ask who prepared the crispy fried chicken, flavorful collard greens, or the delicious Red Velvet cake. It is easy to become hooked on this food. I hope these recipes encourage all cooks to get out the pots and pans and begin preparing the dishes developed by an inherent affinity with recreating feasts that once flourished throughout the Southern region.

SUPPER
AT
RICHARD'S PLACE

Appetizers

APPETIZERS

Growing up in a Southern Baptist household with a father who was a Deacon and a cook meant that friends and neighbors were always stopping by my house. My mother was never really big on entertaining. However, my father loved company and any reason to showcase his culinary skills. Sometimes he would treat his guests to desserts and other times to full course meals. When he did not feel up to a lot of cooking, he simply prepared "finger foods" or hors d'oeuvres as the *fancy folks* called them. Finger foods were simply appetizers that guests ate with one hand and ideally did not require using flatware.

My father could turn a simple visit into a festive occasion. I often think that I am experiencing the exact same feelings as my father did when he brought joy to his friends and family members as they smacked their lips while enjoying his savory snacks. I get great joy creating a party atmosphere using simple ingredients.

Appetizers do not require fancy or expensive ingredients. What I particularly like about appetizers is that they also do not require hours of preparation time. My father rarely used sauces, and he definitely did not use salsas, but I have a feeling that he would enjoy my adaptations on some of his fun foods.

So get out the forks and frilly toothpicks because this chapter provides a wide range of appetizers for mild to spicy palates.

Barbecue Shrimp

The barbecue shrimp is wonderful when served alone or as a topping for a miniature open-faced, toasted buttermilk biscuit. My customers equally enjoy this shrimp recipe with grits or white rice.

2 oz. sweet butter
1 tbsp. grated Spanish onion
1 tsp. minced fresh garlic
2 tbsp. sugar
1 cup Worcestershire sauce
1¼ cup catsup
1 tsp. Dijon mustard
1 tsp. yellow mustard
1 tbsp. white vinegar
½ tsp. jerk seasoning
Salt and pepper, to taste
20 medium shrimp, peeled, cleaned, and deveined

On low heat, melt butter in a medium sauce pan. Add grated onions, garlic, and sugar. Using a wooden spoon, stir mixture well for approximately 3 minutes. Add remaining ingredients except shrimp. Allow sauce to simmer for 8 minutes, stirring occasionally. Add shrimp and cook an additional 5 minutes. Makes 4 servings.

Seasoned Boiled Shrimp with Cocktail Sauce

Shrimp cocktail is an American icon amongst the list of favorite appetizers.

    48 oz. water
    1 tsp. Old Bay seasoning
    1 bay leaf
    1 cup dry white wine
    1 lemon, quartered
    1 rib celery, cut in three pieces
    1 medium carrot, cut in three pieces
    1 medium onion, peeled and cut in half
    20 medium shrimp, peeled, cleaned, and deveined, with tails on.

In a medium pot add all ingredients except shrimp. Bring to a boil, then add shrimp. Cook shrimp for approximately 10 minutes or until shrimp turn pink. Remove shrimp from pot and place in a perforated pan (or colander) on a bed of ice. Allow shrimp to cool. Refrigerate shrimp until ready to use. Serve chilled with cocktail sauce. Makes 4 servings.

Cocktail Sauce

    1 cup chili sauce
    1 tsp. prepared horseradish
    1 tsp. hot sauce
    Juice from 1 lemon, seeds removed

In a small bowl, combine all ingredients. Mix well. Refrigerate for 1 hour. Serve chilled with shrimp. Makes 4 servings.

Cocktail Meatballs

½ lb. ground beef sirloin
½ lb. ground turkey
¼ lb. ground pork
2 tbsp. minced onions
2 tbsp. minced green peppers
1 tsp. minced fresh garlic
¼ cup milk
½ cup plain breadcrumbs
2 large eggs, beaten
Salt and black pepper, to taste
2 cups beef broth

Preheat oven to 350 degrees. Combine all the ingredients except beef broth and mix well. Shape the meat mixture into 24 small meatballs and place the meatballs on a medium baking pan. Pour beef broth into pan. Cover pan with aluminum foil and bake for 20 minutes.

Remove foil from pan after 20 minutes. Cook uncovered meatballs an additional 10 minutes. Serve hot. Makes 6 servings.

Corn and Smoked Oyster Fritters

I always serve these fritters with my special renditions of a remoulade sauce and any one of my salsa sauces. The two sauces create a superb contrast in flavors. This appetizer is a favorite item on the menu. Even customers who are not crazy about the consistency of fresh oysters love the firmness of smoked oysters. In addition to ordering this selection as an appetizer, several of my customers who are vegetarians order the fritters with a few side dishes as an entree. I use fresh corn in season to give these fritters a farm fresh flavor.

These tasty morsels might have played a role in helping one couple tie the knot. This couple frequently dined at the restaurant while dating and immediately fell in love with these fritters. When they booked me to cater their wedding reception, the groom insisted that I include the fritters with the remoulade sauce and tomato salsa as one of their appetizers. Their guests were wild about these flavorful delicacies. Due to the rave reviews, this couple always orders the fritters for all of their family's celebrations.

2 cups whole kernel corn, frozen or cut from the cob
3 tbsp. all-purpose flour
1 tsp. baking powder
1 large egg
1 3.75-oz. can smoked oysters
½ tsp. seafood seasoning
4 oz. canola oil, for frying

In a medium mixing bowl, combine all ingredients except canola oil. Heat oil in a heavy gauge frying pan to 325 degrees. Use a large tablespoon to place fritters in oil. Cook fritters on each side approximately 1½ minutes or until golden brown. Cooking time will depend on size of fritters. Remove fritters from oil and drain on paper towel. Serve hot. Makes 5 servings.

Crab and Fresh Corn Cakes

I recall serving this appetizer at a reception following a movie premiere. This appetizer is mouth watering when served alone or with a variety of sauces and salsas. However, on one occasion, when I served the crab and corn cakes with my black-eyed pea relish, the combination caused quite a buzz amongst the guests. Apparently, they were accustomed to eating black-eyed peas as a side dish on top of rice.

1 lb. lump crab meat, thoroughly picked over to remove cartilage
2 large eggs
2 tsp. Worcestershire sauce
2 tsp. fresh lemon juice
4 oz. whole kernel corn, frozen or cut from the cob
4 oz. finely chopped onion
4 oz. finely chopped bell pepper
1 tsp. Dijon mustard
3 tbsp. mayonnaise
1 cup plain breadcrumbs
1 tsp. seafood seasoning
4 oz. canola oil, for frying

Combine all ingredients except canola oil in a mixing bowl. Using the palms of the hand, shape mixture into patties. Place oil in medium frying pan. Heat oil to 325 degrees and place crab cakes into frying pan. Cook each patty 2 to 3 minutes on each side. Remove crab cakes from frying pan and place each patty on a cookie sheet. Bake in a preheated 350 degree oven for 8 minutes. Remove crab cakes from oven and serve hot with tartar sauce. Makes 4 servings.

Crab Cakes with Mango Salsa

1 lb. lump crab meat, thoroughly picked over to remove cartilage
1 tbsp. mayonnaise
1 egg, beaten
1 tsp. Dijon mustard
1 tsp. chopped fresh parsley
1 tsp. seafood seasoning
¼ cup plain breadcrumbs
Salt and pepper, to taste
Juice from ½ lemon, remove seeds
1 cup vegetable oil, for frying

Place all ingredients except vegetable oil in a medium size mixing bowl. Mix all the ingredients well. Using the palms of the hand, shape crab meat mixture into eight small crab cakes.

Heat oil in a heavy gauge skillet to 325 degrees. Place crab cakes in hot oil and cook approximately 3 minutes on each side. Remove crab cakes from oil and drain on paper towels. Makes 4 servings.

Mango Salsa

2 small mangos
1 tbsp. finely chopped red onion
1 tbsp. finely chopped Vidalia onion
3 tbsp. finely chopped green pepper
2 tbsp. finely chopped fresh cilantro
Juice from 1 lime
Salt and pepper, to taste

Peel mangos and chop into small cubes. In a small bowl, combine all ingredients and mix well. Refrigerate for 1 hour allowing the flavors to blend. Makes 4 servings.

Grilled Black-Eyed-Pea Patties

1 cup dry black-eyed peas, pick over to remove unfavorable particles from peas
5 cups cold water
½ tsp. granulated garlic
1 tbsp. minced onion
3 tbsp. finely chopped tomato
1 pinch turmeric
5 tbsp. chopped cilantro
3 tbsp. fresh lemon juice
1 pinch cayenne pepper
Salt, to taste
4 tbsp. olive oil

Soak peas 3 hours or overnight. Place peas in medium pot with 5 cups of water. Boil peas for 1 hour on medium heat until tender. Drain well and mash peas until semi-smooth. Add remaining ingredients. Using a small scoop, form mixture into approximately 8 to 10 patties. Coat grilling pan with olive oil. Place patties into pan and grill until golden brown on each side. Makes 8 to 10 servings.

Hush Puppies

On occasions when my father was in an especially good mood, he would prepare hush puppies as a special treat to accompany fried fish. First, he fried the fish. Seasoned oil always enhanced the flavor of any fish he fried. Then he used the same oil to fry the hush puppies. Half the fun was popping these corn treats into our mouths. The other pleasure was their taste.

I maintain this tradition and use the same technique when I prepare these hush puppies to serve with fish platters.

1 cup yellow corn meal
2 tsp. baking powder
½ tsp. salt
1 tsp. Cajun spice
½ tsp. cayenne pepper
1 chopped medium onion
¼ cup whole kernel corn, frozen or cut from the cob
2 large eggs
¼ cup buttermilk
8½ oz. vegetable oil

In a medium bowl, mix the dry ingredients, chopped onions, and whole kernel corn. Add eggs and buttermilk. Stir well. Set mixture aside.

Heat oil in medium size iron skillet to 350 degrees. Use a tablespoon to place batter into the oil. Deep fry batter 3 to 5 minutes or until golden brown. Batter should float to the top. Drain hush puppies on paper towel. Serve hot. Makes 4 servings.

Jalapeno Hush Puppies with Crabmeat

2 cups fine yellow corn meal
1 cup self-rising flour
2½ tbsp. sugar
4 tsp. baking powder
1½ tsp. kosher salt
1 cup chopped onion
1½ tbsp. chopped Jalapeno pepper
1½ cup buttermilk
2 large eggs
8 oz. lump crab meat, thoroughly picked over to remove cartilage
3 cups canola oil, for frying

In a medium bowl, combine all ingredients except oil. Preheat oil in a large black cast-iron skillet to 350 degrees. Drop a level tablespoon of batter into hot oil. Cook until golden brown on both sides, approximately 3 minutes. Drain hush puppies on paper towel. Makes 4 servings.

Fried Okra with Lemon Caper Sauce

Customers who typically do not like okra for its texture absolutely enjoy this appetizer because the finished product is firm and crispy. Occasionally, I prepare this dish the same day of serving. However, I have gotten the best results when I marinade the okra in the buttermilk mixture overnight.

2 cups buttermilk
1 tsp. Old Bay seasoning
1 tsp. salt
1 tsp. black pepper
½ tsp. cayenne pepper
1 tbsp. hot sauce
1 lb. medium okra, untrimmed
2½ cups yellow corn meal
1½ cups vegetable oil

In a medium bowl, add buttermilk, Old Bay seasoning, salt, black pepper, cayenne pepper, and hot sauce. Mix well. Add okra. Cover and refrigerate overnight.

When prepared to fry okra, place yellow corn meal in a shallow pan and set aside. Heat vegetable oil in deep frying pan to 325 degrees. Using tongs, remove the okra from the buttermilk mixture and dredge in the yellow corn meal. Fry in small batches until the okra is crispy and golden brown. Drain okra well on paper towels. Serve hot with lemon caper sauce. Makes 5 servings.

Lemon Caper Sauce

1 cup mayonnaise
1 tbsp. grated parmesan cheese
1 tsp. baby capers
2 tbsp. freshly squeezed lemon juice
1 tsp. minced fresh garlic
1 tbsp. hot sauce

In a medium mixing bowl combine all the ingredients and mix well. Refrigerate until ready to use as a dipping sauce for the okra. Makes 5 servings.

Fried Pecan Chicken Fingers

The perfect accompaniment to the fried pecan chicken fingers is a tasty honey-mustard sauce.

1 tsp. kosher salt
1 tsp. white pepper
½ tsp. garlic powder
2 cups plain breadcrumbs
1 cup chopped pecans
3 cups canola oil
2 lb. chicken cutlets, skin removed
1 cup all-purpose flour
2 cups milk
2 large eggs

In a small dish, mix salt, white pepper, and garlic powder and set aside. Combine breadcrumbs and chopped pecans in a medium mixing bowl and set aside. Heat oil in a heavy skillet on low heat while prepping chicken.

Cut chicken cutlets into strips approximately the size of average fingers. Season chicken with spice mixture, then dredge chicken fingers in flour. Shake off excess flour. Set aside. Blend milk and eggs in a medium bowl. Dip floured chicken fingers in egg mixture and then into breadcrumb and pecan mixture. Set aside until all chicken fingers are thoroughly coated.

Heat oil to 350 degrees when ready to fry chicken. Fry chicken fingers approximately 3 minutes until golden brown. Serve hot or at room temperature with dipping sauce. Makes 4 to 6 servings.

Miniature Orange Corn Muffins with Cranberry and Pear Relish

Several years ago, I catered a record release party for a legendary recording artist who played a guitar and sang the blues. These muffins served with thinly sliced smoked ham were his favorite appetizer. He was so impressed with the combination of flavors that he asked if he could take a picture with me! This was definitely a proud moment.

These muffins are always a hit with guests whenever I cater upscale parties. I also use sliced smoked turkey in place of ham, based upon the customer's preference.

2½ cups all-purpose flour
2½ cups yellow corn meal
5 tsp. baking powder
1¼ tsp. baking soda
1½ cups fine sugar
2½ tsp. salt
1 cup milk
2 cups orange juice
6 large eggs
8 oz. vegetable oil
8 oz. unsalted melted butter
24 pieces thinly sliced ham

Preheat oven to 325 degrees. In a medium bowl, mix all dry ingredients and set aside. In a small bowl, blend milk and orange juice. Add liquid mixture to dry mixture.

In a separate bowl, beat eggs slightly and then add to mixture. Mix batter well. Add vegetable oil and melted butter to batter. Beat well and set aside.

Spray mini muffin pan with baking release spray. Using a teaspoon, fill each insert in muffin pan with batter. Bake in 325 degree oven for 15 to 20 minutes or until golden brown. Muffin is ready if a toothpick inserted into the middle comes out clean. Makes 8 servings.

Cranberry and Pear Relish

1 cup cold water
1 cup whole cranberries
½ cup brown sugar
¾ cup white sugar
1 Bartlett pear, peeled and diced to small cubes

Place all ingredients in a heavy quart sauce pan. Cook on medium heat for 15 minutes. Cranberries should pop open. Remove from heat and cool until ready to use.

Slice muffins in half separating the top of each muffin from the bottom half. Place a few pieces of thinly sliced ham or smoked turkey with a smear of relish on the bottom half of muffin. Replace tops of muffins and insert decorative toothpicks to hold miniature sandwiches together. Makes 8 servings.

Oyster Fritters

1 pt. shucked fresh oysters, reserve ½ cup juice from oysters
2 cups all-purpose flour
¼ tsp. baking soda
¼ tsp. cayenne pepper
¼ tsp. Old Bay seasoning
salt and pepper, to taste
3 eggs, beaten
¼ cup buttermilk
½ cup oyster juice
1 qt. vegetable oil, for frying

Chop oysters into medium size pieces. Set aside. In a small bowl, combine flour, baking soda, cayenne pepper, Old Bay seasoning, salt, and pepper. In another bowl, combine eggs, milk, and oyster juice.

Heat oil in a frying skillet to 325 degrees. Using a tablespoon, drop batter into oil. Cook fritters for 3 minutes on each side. Remove from oil and drain on paper towels. Serve with tartar sauce or remoulade sauce. Makes 8 servings.

Deep Fried Cajun Oysters

Whenever I prepare this recipe, I purchase fresh oysters already shucked and drained from my fish monger. This convenience saves an immeasurable amount of time and diminishes my concerns that novice cooks will hurt themselves preparing this appetizer if unfamiliar with the technique of removing the oyster from the shell.

Prior to preparing the oysters, I insist that my sous-chef allocates a few extra minutes to prepare tartar sauce using my recipe and refrigerate until ready to use. It may be tempting to buy tartar sauce already bottled. However, I do not compromise taste to save a minimal amount of time.

½ cup buttermilk
½ cup milk
2 eggs, beaten
8 oz. all-purpose flour
8 oz. yellow corn meal
2½ tbsp. Cajun spice mix
2 cups canola oil
1 lb. oysters, shucked and drained

Combine buttermilk, milk, and eggs. Mix well and set aside. In a small bowl, mix flour, corn meal, and Cajun spice. Combine well. Set aside. Heat oil in cast iron frying pan to 350 degrees.

Dip oysters in milk mixture. Dredge in seasoned flour and corn meal mix. Place oysters in hot oil. Fry for approximately 3 to 4 minutes or until golden brown. Drain oysters on paper towel. Serve hot with tartar sauce. Makes 4 servings.

Potato Pancakes with Apple Sauce

I find that these pancakes are popular with diverse populations. Due to its wide appeal, I suggest them as appetizers when catering parties with multicultural guests. When cooking for affluent clientele, I substitute sour cream and caviar in place of apple sauce.

> 3 medium russet potatoes
> 2 tbsp. grated onions
> 1 medium egg
> 1 pinch grated nutmeg
> 1 tbsp. all-purpose flour
> salt and pepper, to taste
> 2 cups vegetable oil

Peel and grate potatoes. Place grated potatoes in a clean kitchen towel and squeeze out all liquid. Add onions, egg, flour, and seasonings.

Heat oil in a large frying pan to 350 degrees. Using a tablespoon, drop mixture in hot oil, making 8 pancakes. Cook pancakes for 2 minutes on each side. Makes 4 servings.

Apple Sauce

> 2 golden apples, peeled and diced
> ¼ cup apple juice
> ¼ tsp. ground cinnamon
> 2 tbsp. sugar

Combine all ingredients in small sauce pan. Simmer on low heat for 10 to 15 minutes until apples are tender. Cool and serve with potato pancakes. Makes 4 servings.

Spicy Wings with Blue Cheese Dip

Certain customers who enjoy eating "hot" food prefer to eat these wings without the blue cheese dip. The flavor is very powerful. Therefore I suggest serving the wings with the dip for most guests who have a milder palate.

> 8 chicken wings, tips removed
> 1 cup all-purpose flour
> 2 cups vegetable oil
> 4 oz. unsalted butter
> 4 oz. hot sauce
> 4 oz. dry white wine
> 1 tsp. minced fresh garlic
> 1 tbsp. fresh chopped cilantro

Cut each chicken wing at the joint into 2 separate pieces. Dredge each piece in flour. Shake off excess flour and set aside. In a medium frying pan, heat vegetable oil to 350 degrees. Fry chicken pieces in vegetable oil for approximately 15 minutes or until golden brown. Chicken is ready when the pieces float to the top of the oil. Remove each piece of chicken from oil and drain on paper towel. Set aside.

In a medium sauce pan, combine butter, hot sauce, wine, garlic, and cilantro. Cook ingredients on medium heat. When butter mixture begins to boil, add chicken pieces. Coat pieces well with butter mixture. Reduce heat and simmer approximately 3 minutes. Remove pan from heat and serve chicken pieces sizzling with blue cheese dip. Makes 4 servings.

Blue Cheese Dip

> 6 oz. mayonnaise
> 2 tsp. sour cream
> 2 oz. crumbled gorgonzola blue cheese

Combine all ingredients and mix well. Refrigerate 30 minutes. Serve with spicy wings. Makes 4 servings.

Soups and Salads

SOUPS AND SALADS

Warm bowls of soup nourish the body and warm the soul on the cold winter days that we experience during the winter months in the North. Contrary to popular belief, there are a number of soups that do not consume a tremendous amount of time. I always use various combinations of vegetables, shellfish, meat, or poultry to quickly create excellent soups. While some soups do require simmering for a period of time, they do not need constant attention and the process builds in the flavor.

I have some customers who order soup and salad for their meal. When they add a piece of bread to their order they experience a totally satisfying meal. I do not get a lot of requests for cold soups. Even during the summer months, my customers prefer a warm bowl of this sustenance. I tend to change some of the daily specials during the summer months when heartier salads often serve as a main course during this season.

Anyone can make a great salad using a variety of fresh salad greens, herbs, and fine dressings. I eat a salad once a day topped with red onions and a vinaigrette or creamy dressing. I prefer using mixed greens and a variety of vegetables grilled and roasted, which I prepare more often for catered events. Many of my customers who dine at the restaurant still prefer a basic salad consisting of iceberg lettuce, cucumbers, tomatoes, and a sprinkling of shredded carrots. Therefore, I have included a range for all tastes.

I serve an awful lot of potato salad and coleslaw throughout the year. My customers are very particular about their potato salad and coleslaw, so I take great pride in knowing that they adore this Southern standard. I hope all of the salads are winners.

Chicken Vegetable Soup

1 tbsp. extra virgin olive oil
1 tbsp. unsalted butter
2 chicken cutlets, cubed
Salt and pepper to taste
2 white potatoes, peeled and diced
½ cup chopped celery
½ cup peeled and sliced carrots
½ cup finely chopped Spanish onion
½ tsp. minced fresh garlic
48 oz. chicken broth
1 bay leaf
1 tbsp. chopped flat parsley, for garnish

Place a medium pot over low heat. Add olive oil and butter. Allow butter to melt. Season chicken with salt and pepper to taste. Add chicken to pot and sauté approximately 4 minutes. Add potatoes, vegetables and garlic. Sauté for approximately 3 additional minutes. Reduce heat to a low simmer. Add chicken broth and bay leaf. Simmer soup for approximately 20 minutes. Remove bay leaf. Garnish soup with chopped parsley just before serving. Makes 4 to 6 servings.

Split Pea Soup

4 cups dried split peas, picked over to remove unwanted particles
2 tbsp. olive oil
2 lb. smoked beef sausage; remove skin and slice into small pieces
2 medium onions, chopped small
1 cup finely chopped carrots
½ cup finely chopped celery
1 tbsp. minced fresh garlic
1 bay leaf
3 qt. chicken stock, heated
1 cup heavy cream
Salt and pepper to taste

Soak peas 2 hours. Set aside. Place medium pot on low heat. Add oil, sausage, and onions. Sauté 5 minutes. Add carrots, garlic, and bay leaf. Continue to cook approximately 3 minutes. Add chicken stock and peas. Cover pot. Simmer soup for 55 minutes, stirring often. Be careful not to let soup stick or burn. Stir in cream. Season with salt and pepper. Serve hot. Makes 8-10 servings.

Vegetable Soup

2 tbsp. vegetable oil
1 cup chopped carrots
1 cup chopped celery
½ cup chopped onion
1 clove minced garlic
2 cups shredded green cabbage
1½ qt. chicken stock
1 14½-oz can stewed tomatoes
1 sprig rosemary
1 tsp. parsley chopped
Salt and pepper to taste

In a 4-qt. pot over medium heat, combine oil, carrots, celery, onions, garlic, and cabbage and sauté approximately 3 minutes. Add chicken stock, tomatoes, herbs, and salt and pepper. Turn heat to a simmer and cook for 20 minutes. Makes 8 servings.

Apple and Walnut Salad

1 Red Delicious apple, cored and chopped
1 yellow apple, cored and chopped
1 Granny Smith apple, cored and chopped
¼ cup dark raisins
¼ cup chopped celery
¼ cup chopped walnuts
¾ cup vanilla yogurt
1 tsp. honey

In a small bowl combine all the ingredients together and mix well. Refrigerate until ready to serve. Makes 8 servings.

Black-Eyed-Pea Salad with Vinaigrette Dressing

A staple in the Southern diet for more than 300 years, black-eyed peas have long been associated with good luck. A dish of peas is a New Year's tradition in most areas of the South, thought to bring prosperity for the new year. When I initially began cooking, I always served black-eyed peas as a warm side dish topping white rice. Over the years, through much experimentation, I now equally enjoy using this pea in salads, relishes, and in patties.

2 cups dry black-eyed peas, picked over to remove unwanted particles
2 qt. water
½ cup chopped red pepper
½ cup chopped green pepper
½ cup cherry tomatoes, halved
½ cup chopped celery
1 Jalapeno pepper, seeded and sliced
½ cup chopped red onion
1 qt. fresh cilantro

Soak the black-eyed peas in water for 4 hours. Drain and rinse peas. Cook peas in a medium pot on low heat for approximately 25 to 30 minutes or until peas are tender. Strain peas. Allow to cool. In a medium bowl, mix cool peas with chopped vegetables. Set aside. Use Vinaigrette Dressing. Makes 8-10 servings.

Vinaigrette Dressing

½ cup red vinegar
¼ cup balsamic vinegar
1 tbsp. Dijon mustard
2 tbsp. sugar
1 tbsp. honey
1½ cups extra virgin olive oil
½ tsp. fresh chopped garlic
Salt and pepper to taste
2 tbsp. chopped flat leaf parsley, to use as optional garnish

Place all ingredients in a mixing bowl or blender. Mix well for approximately 3 minutes. Pour dressing over Black-Eyed Pea Salad. Refrigerate for approximately 20 minutes before serving. Serve chilled. If desired, garnish with chopped parsley. Makes 8 to 10 servings.

Roasted Beets, Goat Cheese, and Red Onion Salad

4 medium fresh beets
1 red medium onion
8 oz. goat cheese

Preheat oven to 325 degrees. Wrap each beet in aluminum foil and bake for 1 hour and 20 minutes or until tender. Allow beets to cool. Peel beets and slice thinly. Thinly slice onions. Arrange beets and onions on a platter. Top with crumbled goat cheese. Refrigerate until ready to use. The Truffle Vinaigrette Dressing is an excellent choice for this salad. Makes 6 servings.

Truffle Vinaigrette Dressing

4 oz. truffle oil
3 oz. red wine vinegar
1 oz. olive oil
½ tsp. Dijon mustard
1 tsp. sugar

In a medium bowl, combine all ingredients together and whisk well. Refrigerate until ready to use. Makes 6 servings.

Carrot Salad

3 cups shredded carrots
¼ cup pineapple juice
¼ cup golden raisins
½ tsp. ground cinnamon
¾ cup mayonnaise

In a medium bowl combine all ingredients together and mix well. Refrigerate for 1 hour before serving. Makes 6 servings.

Coleslaw

5 cups shredded green cabbage
¾ cup shredded carrots
2½ tbsp. sugar
¾ cup mayonnaise
¼ cup sour cream
2 tbsp. white vinegar
1 tbsp. minced onion

In a medium bowl, combine all the ingredients together. Refrigerate for 1 hour before serving. Makes 12 servings.

Creamy Coleslaw

Coleslaws always make me think about the fun-filled barbecues I have enjoyed throughout my life. They are an excellent substitute for lettuce salads. I commonly use green cabbage and, when I want to add color, I also use red cabbage.

1 head green cabbage
½ green pepper, finely diced
¼ medium onion, grated
1 medium carrot, shredded
2 cups mayonnaise
¼ cup buttermilk
½ cup sugar
¼ cup white vinegar
Salt and pepper to taste

Shred cabbage in a large bowl. Add diced pepper, grated onion, and shredded carrot. Mix in mayonnaise, buttermilk, sugar and vinegar. Refrigerate for 30 minutes before serving. Makes 8 servings.

Georgia Peach Salad

4 fresh Georgia peaches, halved and pitted
1 tsp. walnut oil
3 tbsp. peach nectar
2 tbsp. balsamic vinegar
2 tbsp. olive oil
Salt and pepper to taste
4 cups mixed salad greens
2 oz. crumbled goat cheese
½ red onion, thinly sliced
¼ cup chopped pecans

Heat frying pan with grill marks on medium heat. Brush peaches with walnut oil. Grill peaches skin side up for approximately 3 minutes. Set aside. Combine peach nectar, vinegar, and olive oil. Season with salt and pepper to taste. Whisk well. Refrigerate until ready to use.

On a medium platter, arrange nicely salad greens, grilled peach halves, goat cheese, onions, and chopped pecans. Pour Peach Vinaigrette over salad. Makes 4 servings.

Potato Salad

2½ lb. baking potatoes, peeled, cooked, and medium chopped
1 green bell pepper, chopped small
1¼ cup celery, chopped small
½ cup sweet pickle relish
¾ cup sweet mixed pickles, chopped small
¼ cup minced onion
2 tbsp. sugar
3 hard boiled eggs, chopped small
1 tbsp. Dijon mustard
1 cup mayonnaise
2 tbsp. white vinegar
Salt and black pepper to taste

In a medium bowl, combine potatoes, bell pepper, celery, relish, pickles, and onions. Mix well. Add sugar, eggs, mustard, mayonnaise, vinegar, salt and black pepper. Mix well. Refrigerate for 1 hour before serving. Makes 12 servings.

Tomato, Onion, and Basil Salad

3 medium beefsteak tomatoes
1 small red onion
6 basil leaves, cut in strips
3 oz. extra virgin olive oil
1 oz. balsamic vinegar
Salt and pepper to taste

Slice tomatoes and onions in rings. Arrange on a platter. Add salt and pepper. Drizzle with oil and vinegar. Makes 6 servings.

Fish and Seafood

FISH AND SEAFOOD

Throughout the years, one thing that I have learned is not to take anything for granted, especially when it comes to food. My wife often reminds me that not *everyone* shares the same passion for spending endless hours researching information about food and cooking techniques as I do. Therefore, for the novice cook, I would like to take a few minutes to offer a brief description to clarify the difference between the term fish and shellfish.

Although many restaurant menus and cookbooks often group fish and shellfish together under the term "seafood," there is a difference. Fish have fins and internal skeletons and shellfish have outer shells but no internal bone structure. Also, there is a wide variety of fish that live in rivers, streams, lakes, and ponds.

This information is somewhat important, because there were so many types of fish, each with their own characteristics and cooking requirements. Some familiarity about their basic structure is helpful because each type of fish requires a particular way for handling and cooking. When preparing fish, regardless of its type, keep in mind that:

1. Fish is very delicate and cooks very quickly even at a low temperature
2. Fish is naturally tender
3. Handle cooked fish very carefully or it will fall apart

The flesh of cooked fish breaks apart when pierced with a fork; cooks refer to this as "flaking." This does not mean that the fish should fall apart easily. When fish falls apart easily, I know that it's overdone. As with meat and poultry, fish also retains its heat and continues to cook after being removed from heat. Keeping these few tips in mind will help to preserve moistness and prevent overcooking.

I love shellfish, and so do most of my customers. For that reason, I serve a large amount of entrees that offer a combination of shrimp and chicken, shrimp and ribs, and seafood platters. On special occasions I feature lobster specials.

Two of my favorite types of fish are catfish and whiting. To save time and to cut down on labor costs, I purchase the fish already filleted. Whiting is a lean, firm-textured, and delicately flavored fish. I only serve fresh whiting, although frozen whiting is available.

Catfish is also low in fat with firm white meat. Mark Twain

once said that "Catfish is a plenty good enough fish for anyone." Well, I remember when I first opened my restaurant, I had a very hard time selling catfish. Many of my customers did not know that most of the catfish sold in restaurants is farm raised in hatcheries. So many of my customers shared their stories about their childhood memories and catfish while apologizing for not ordering this fish. Many of them had fathers or grandfathers who they believed fished in "creeks" and returned with an unattractive fish with "whiskers!" They did not want any part of eating catfish. In order to change my customers' opinions about catfish, I spent numerous hours informing them about fish hatcheries, and how I only cooked fillets.

I thank God for the customers who trusted my judgment and ordered the catfish. Over a period of time, as customers saw this beautifully golden-fried fish on other customer's plates and heard the rave reviews, they too began ordering catfish.

I now serve catfish fried, broiled, barbecued, stuffed with crabmeat, and blackened. Catfish is a very versatile fish that is rich in flavor. Catfish don't have scales and most chefs usually remove the skin of this fish before frying or broiling. I try to keep enough on hand because now if I run out, my customers are ready to revolt.

Although I have a fondness for catfish and whiting, the following section offers a range of seafood and cooking styles and various seasonings and sauces to please any seafood lover's taste.

Baked Salmon Fillet

4 6-oz. salmon fillets
Salt and black pepper to taste
4 oz. melted unsalted butter
4 oz. dry white wine
2 flat anchovies, minced

Place salmon on a medium baking dish. Season with salt and pepper. Set aside. In a small mixing bowl, combine butter, wine and anchovies. Stir well.

Pour butter mixture over salmon and bake 12 minutes. Remove salmon from oven. Top with pesto sauce to enhance the flavor of the fish. Makes 4 servings.

Baked Stuffed Salmon with Crabmeat Stuffing

4 5-oz. salmon fillets, pin bones removed
Salt and black pepper to taste
4 oz. melted unsalted butter
1 tbsp. paprika
4 lemon wedges

Preheat oven to 375 degrees. Season salmon with salt and pepper. Place salmon in shallow baking dish, skin down, and set aside.

Place 2 scoops of Crabmeat Stuffing the length of the salmon. Using your hands, pat the stuffing down to flatten. Pour butter over the stuffed salmon and sprinkle with paprika. Cook for 15 minutes or until fish flakes when tested with a fork. Serve salmon hot and garnish with lemon wedge. Makes 4 servings.

Crabmeat Stuffing

I use this recipe when I stuff salmon, catfish, lobster, and shrimp. I have a few customers who love the taste of this stuffing so much that they often order an additional amount as a side dish. This stuffing can turn a basic broiled fish dish into a special event.

½ lb. unsalted butter
1 medium onion, chopped small
1 green pepper, chopped small
1 lb. lump Crabmeat, picked over to remove cartilage
2 tbsp. Worcestershire sauce
3 tbsp. mayonnaise
1 tbsp. Dijon mustard
1 tsp. seafood seasoning
Juice from 1 lemon, remove seeds
2 large eggs, beaten
8 oz. plain white cracker crumbs
Salt and black pepper to taste

Melt butter in small pot on medium heat. Add onions and peppers. Cook for 4 minutes. Add crabmeat, Worcestershire sauce, mayonnaise, mustard, seafood seasoning, lemon juice, eggs, and cracker crumbs. Mix well and cook for an additional 4 minutes. Remove from heat and season with salt and pepper. Cool before stuffing salmon. Makes 4 servings.

Baked Salmon Steak

4 6-oz. salmon steaks
Kosher salt to taste
Black pepper to taste
Juice from 1 lemon, seeds removed
4 oz. melted unsalted butter
4 oz. dry white wine
1 tbsp. minced fresh garlic
1 tbsp. chopped fresh parsley
1 tbsp. Spanish paprika
4 lemon wedges

Preheat oven to 375 degrees. Squeeze lemon juice on each salmon steak. Place salmon steaks in shallow baking dish. Season salmon with salt and pepper. Set aside.

Combine lemon juice, butter, wine, garlic, and parsley in small bowl and mix well. Pour mixture over salmon and sprinkle each salmon with paprika. Cook salmon in oven for 15 minutes or until salmon flakes when tested with a fork. Serve hot and garnish with lemon wedge. Makes 4 servings.

Poached Fillet of Salmon

Poaching is an excellent way of preparing fish for those individuals who are watching their weight. This method entails cooking the fish in water, wine, or another seasoned liquid at a very low heat that is hot but not actually bubbling, approximately 160 degrees. However, for those who feel free to indulge in a few extra calories, this fish is quite elegant with a dollop of herb mayonnaise.

1 cup dry white wine
2 carrots, peeled and diced
2 bay leaves
Salt and white pepper to taste
Sprig of thyme
Juice from 1 lemon
10 cups water
½ cup diced celery
1 lb. salmon fillet, cut in 4 oz. pieces

In a medium saucepan, combine all ingredients except the salmon. Simmer liquid for approximately 15 minutes. Carefully place the salmon with the skin down in the liquid. The liquid should completely cover the fish. Poach the salmon approximately 10 to 15 minutes. When the salmon is done, carefully remove the fish from liquid. Allow fish to cool for 30 minutes. Serve chilled with or without Herb Mayonnaise. Makes 4 servings.

Herb Mayonnaise

1 cup mayonnaise
Juice from 1 lemon
¼ cup watercress, no stems
¼ cup fresh dill
1 tsp. minced garlic
½ tsp. minced anchovies
Salt and pepper to taste

In a food processor, mix all ingredients together for approximately 2 minutes or until the mixture is smooth. Remove the mixture from the food processor and refrigerate until ready to serve. Makes 4 servings.

Spice Mixture for Blackened Fish

Most supermarkets sell pre-packaged seasonings for blackening fish, meat, and poultry. I have tried several of these seasonings, but prefer this freshly-made mixture. I suggest using this recipe when blackening fish or any other food.

    3 tsp. paprika
    1 tsp. cayenne pepper
    1 tsp. black pepper
    1 tsp. dried thyme
    1 tsp. kosher salt
    1 tsp. onion powder
    1 tsp. garlic powder

Place all ingredients in a small bowl and mix well. Makes 6 servings.

Blackened Salmon

    2 oz. unsalted melted butter
    2 tbsp. olive oil
    4 6-oz. salmon fillets
    Spice mixture to taste

Combine butter and olive oil in cast-iron skillet on medium-high heat. Season salmon with spice mixture on both sides. Place salmon in skillet, skin side up, for 3 minutes. Turn salmon and cook for an additional 3 minutes on the other side or until fish flakes when tested with a fork. When customers prefer their fish well done, I cook the salmon for a few extra minutes on each side. Serve hot. Makes 4 servings.

Blackened Catfish Fillet

3 oz. vegetable oil
2 9-oz. catfish fillets
Spice mixture to taste

Place vegetable oil in cast iron skillet on medium high heat. Season catfish with spice mixture on both sides. Place catfish in hot skillet about 5 minutes on both sides. Serve hot. Makes 4 servings.

Fried Catfish

4 6-oz. catfish fillets
Salt and pepper to taste
1 cup buttermilk
1 cup milk
2 large eggs
1 lb. yellow cornmeal
2 cups canola oil
4 lemon wedges

Rinse pieces of fillet catfish quickly in cold water. Pat dry. Season fish with salt and pepper. Combine buttermilk, milk, and eggs. Beat ingredients well. Add salt and pepper to cornmeal. Heat oil in iron skillet at about 350 degrees. Dip fish in egg wash and then in cornmeal. Pan fry fish in hot oil until golden brown. Drain oil from fish on paper towel. Garnish with lemon wedges before serving. Makes 4 servings

Grilled Catfish

4 7-oz. catfish fillets
4 tsp. olive oil
1 tsp. garlic powder
½ tsp. cracked black pepper
¼ tsp. ground cayenne pepper
1 tsp. kosher salt

Preheat cast-iron skillet with grill marks on medium heat. Brush each fillet with olive oil on both sides. Set fillets aside.

Combine garlic powder, cracked black pepper, ground cayenne, and kosher salt. Sprinkle spices on each piece of catfish seasoning both sides with mixture.

Lightly brush cast iron skillet with olive oil. Place 2 pieces of catfish in skillet on medium heat and grill 4 minutes on each side. Remove fillets, place on pan, and put in a 200-degree oven to keep hot.

Brush skillet lightly with olive oil. Grill remaining 2 pieces of catfish the same amount of time using the same method. Serve hot with Watermelon Salsa. Makes 4 servings.

Pecan Catfish

4 7-oz. catfish fillets
Salt and black pepper to taste
2 cups milk
2 large eggs
1 cup plain breadcrumbs
½ cup finely chopped pecans
2½ cups vegetable oil

Season catfish with salt and pepper. Set aside. In a medium bowl, combine eggs and milk. Stir well. Set aside. In a medium pan, combine breadcrumbs and pecans.

Heat oil in large frying pan to 350 degrees. Dip fish in egg mixture and then into breadcrumb mixture. Fry fillets 8 minutes on each side. Remove from oil and drain on paper towel. Makes 4 servings.

Potato-Crusted Catfish

2 7-oz. catfish fillets
Salt and pepper to taste
2 oz. shredded Russet potatoes
1 oz. shredded sweet potatoes
½ oz. shredded Spanish onions
1 egg, beaten
2 tbsp. canola oil
1 cup fish stock
1 tbsp. Dijon mustard
4 oz. Balsamic vinegar
Slices of lemon and limes, for garnish

Season both sides of catfish with salt and pepper. Mix together Russet potatoes and sweet potatoes. Using both hands, place potatoes in palms of hands, and squeeze the water out of potatoes. Place potatoes into a mixing bowl. Add onions to potatoes and mix well. Season mixture with salt and pepper. Brush fish with beaten egg. Spread potato mixture on top of fish. Place oil in medium saucepan on medium heat. When pan is hot, place the fish with potato side down in the pan. Cook fish until potato side is brown. Turn fish to the other side. Cook on the other side for 2 minutes. Remove fish and saucepan from heat. Place fish in a baking pan. Cook in a 350-degree oven for 12 minutes. Return saucepan to medium heat. Add fish stock, mustard, and vinegar. Stir mixture. Cook for approximately 4 minutes. Strain and spoon over fish. Pour $1/4$ of the sauce on the bottom of one plate and $1/4$ of the sauce on the other plate. Pour the remaining sauce on the top of the two pieces of fish. Makes 2 servings.

Stewed Catfish

4 6-oz. pieces of catfish, fillet
2 tbsp. vegetable oil
2 14½-oz. cans of stewed tomatoes
4 oz. julienne onions
4 oz. julienne peppers
½ tsp. minced garlic
1½ tsp. sugar
1 tsp. chopped anchovies
1 tbsp. white vinegar
1 bay leaf
2 cups chicken stock, canned broth, or fresh stock
Fresh black pepper to taste
Salt to taste

Season catfish with salt and pepper. Refrigerate until needed. Using low heat, add vegetable oil to medium saucepan. Add julienne onions. Cook approximately 1 minute until onions are tender. Add minced garlic and cook an additional minute. Add stewed tomatoes, sugar, chopped anchovies, vinegar, bay leaf, and chicken stock. Simmer for approximately 10 to 15 minutes. Add julienne green peppers. Cook an additional 5 minutes. Remove sauce from heat. Place catfish in casserole dish. Spoon tomato mixture over fish. Cover and bake in 350-degree oven for approximately 20 to 25 minutes or until catfish flakes when tested with a fork.

Crabmeat dumplings are a bang-up addition to this dish. Makes 4 servings.

Stuffed Catfish

For customers who prefer eating catfish to salmon, here is my recipe for stuffed catfish. Use my recipe for the Crabmeat Stuffing.

    4 8-oz. catfish fillets
    Salt and pepper to taste
    4 oz. melted unsalted butter
    4 oz. white wine
    ½ tsp. Spanish paprika
    2 tbsp. chopped fresh parsley

Preheat oven to 350 degrees. Season catfish with salt and pepper. Set aside. Combine butter and white wine. Set aside. Place each fillet flat on a countertop or table. Starting from the center of the fish turn the knife so that it is almost parallel to the counter top or table. Leaving the fish flat on countertop, make a 2-inch slit horizontally on the right and left side of the fish creating a pocket for the stuffing. Set aside. Make the Crabmeat Stuffing.

Stuff each of the fillets creating a mound in the center of the pocket. Place each fillet in a shallow baking dish with the stuffing side faced up. Sprinkle butter and wine mixture over the fish. Top each piece of fish with sprinkles of paprika and chopped parsley.

Bake in preheated oven for 20 minutes until the stuffing is browned and the flesh of the fish flakes when tested with a fork. Makes 4 servings.

Baked Tilapia Topped with Peppers and Onions

Tilapia became a popular choice of fish in restaurants approximately 10 years ago. This firm and flaky-textured fish has a sweet flavor. Tilapia is also a very versatile fish that is easily prepared whether baked, blackened, stewed, or grilled.

>4-6 oz. Tilapia fillets, skin and pin bones removed
>Salt and black pepper to taste
>4 oz. unsalted butter
>1 green pepper, cut into thin strips
>1 red pepper, cut into thin strips
>1 sweet onion, cut into thin strips
>1 tbsp. minced fresh garlic

Season fish with salt and pepper. Place fish in shallow baking dish and top with 3 oz. of butter. Cook for 15 minutes or until fish flakes when tested with a fork. While fish is baking, in a medium sauté pan combine the butter, pepper, and garlic. Sauté for about 10 minutes on medium heat.

Remove pan from heat and set aside. Remove fish from oven and top with pepper and onion mixture. Serve hot. Roasted potatoes are a great accompaniment. Makes 4 servings.

Baked Swordfish Fillets

4 6-oz. swordfish fillets
Salt and pepper to taste
1 tbsp. olive oil
3 tbsp. fresh lemon juice
1 tsp. minced fresh garlic
1 tsp. chopped fresh rosemary
1 tsp. chopped fresh thyme
1 tsp. chopped fresh sage

Preheat oven to 375 degrees. Season swordfish with salt and pepper. Place in a shallow baking dish and set aside.

Combine olive oil, lemon juice, garlic, rosemary, thyme, and sage. Mix well and pour over swordfish. Cook in oven for 15 minutes or until fish flakes when tested with a fork. Remove fish from oven. Serve hot. Makes 4 servings.

Baked Barbecue Tuna Steak

This dish is characteristic of a piquant blend of Caribbean and Southern cooking. The result is heavenly.

4 6-oz. tuna steaks, fresh
Salt and black pepper to taste
4 oz. unsalted butter, melted
6 oz. Worcestershire sauce
1 tsp. minced fresh garlic
½ tsp. jerk seasoning
1½ tsp. Dijon mustard
8 oz. catsup
2 tbsp. balsamic vinegar
2 tbsp. fresh chopped parsley, for garnish

Preheat oven to 375 degrees. Place tuna in a shallow baking dish. Season tuna with salt and pepper. Set aside. In a medium bowl, combine butter, Worcestershire sauce, garlic, jerk seasoning, mustard, catsup, and vinegar. Mix well. Spoon barbecue mixture over tuna steaks and bake 12 to 15 minutes. Sprinkle tuna with parsley and serve hot. Makes 4 servings.

Cajun Fried Shrimp

12 large shrimp
Cajun spice
2 cups canola oil
1 cup buttermilk
1 cup milk
2 large eggs
½ lb. yellow cornmeal
½ lb. all-purpose flour

Peel shrimp, leaving tail and one section of shell on shrimp. Devein shrimp by slicing halfway through the back and remove vein. Rinse shrimp after deveining. Open to form butterfly. Beat eggs and milk together. Add buttermilk. Mix well. Combine yellow cornmeal and flour. Coat shrimp with Cajun spice. Dip shrimp in egg and milk mixture. Bread shrimp with cornmeal and flour mixture. Heat canola oil in medium frying pan. When oil reaches 350 degrees, fry shrimp for about 3 to 5 minutes until golden brown. Makes 4 servings.

Shrimp in Scampi Sauce

8 oz. melted unsalted butter
4 oz. dry white wine
2 oz. extra virgin olive oil
3 tbsp. minced fresh garlic
2 tbsp. chopped fresh parsley
Salt and black pepper to taste
Juice from 1 lemon, seeds removed
16 large shrimp, peeled, deveined, and butterflied.
   Leave tail on.

Preheat oven to 375 degrees. Combine melted butter, wine, olive oil, parsley, salt, pepper, and lemon juice. Blend ingredients well. Set aside.
Place shrimp in a shallow baking dish. Pour butter mixture over shrimp and bake 15 minutes until shrimp turn pink. Makes 4 servings.

Fish and Seafood

Curry Shrimp

Whenever I prepare this dish, I recall catering a special meeting at a home of a major film producer and director, and his executive staff. Although I had previously catered several other affairs for this individual, I minimally interacted with him. At the time, I understood that one of his idiosyncrasies was to maintain a "safe distance" from persons apart from his immediate circle. In reviewing the menu with his production manager, she informed me that he "loved" curry shrimp and asked if I prepared the dish. I reassured her that her director would thoroughly enjoy my curry shrimp.

While preparing the meal in the director's kitchen, he entered the kitchen and asked if I was preparing a curry dish. The pungent aroma filled his home. He then asked if he could lift the lid off the saucepan to see what I was cooking. His eyes lit up when he saw the curry shrimp. He smiled from ear to ear and began talking incessantly. He seemed extremely excited and asked me if he could help me in any way. He could not get beyond the smell of the food. I became caught up in his excitement and began sharing the recipe.

Without a second thought, I retrieved a plate from his cupboard, placed a serving of rice on the plate and topped the rice with the curry shrimp. The director laughed and said he really wanted to eat a dish before his staff arrived, but did not want to appear starved. This was definitely a bonding moment.

Food has always served as an essential variable for bridging interpersonal gaps or solidifying relationships for me throughout my career. Regardless of an individual's background, good food always seems to bring people together. Some evenings when I walk into my dining room, I see individuals who represent cultures from many continents.

Cooking for a multicultural clientele requires that I use a broader range of seasonings rather than sticking to the traditional taste of salt and pepper. I often surprise my customers when I prepare daily specials that infuse new herbs and spices with traditional food items.

Curry powder is a blend of many spices. Turmeric is the primary ingredient. However, many curries also often include a careful blend of chili, coriander, cumin, ginger, pepper, and cinnamon. Using curry can change an average food preparation to an exotic dish. I highly recommend this dish for individuals who want to add a little zip to their dish.

4 tbsp. melted unsalted butter
1 medium onion, finely chopped
1 tsp. minced fresh garlic
4 tbsp. all-purpose flour
2 tbsp. curry powder
2 cups coconut milk, heated
1 tsp. minced Scotch bonnet chili pepper
24 large shrimp, peeled, deveined, and washed
2 tbsp. chopped fresh cilantro

Place butter in a large saucepan over low heat. Add the onion and garlic and cook for 3 minutes. Stir in the flour and curry powder. Cook for an additional 5 minutes.

Whisk in coconut milk. Continue to whisk until sauce is smooth and thick. Add minced chili pepper. Stir into mixture. Add shrimp and simmer for 6 minutes or until shrimp are cooked. Garnish shrimp curry with cilantro and serve hot with white rice or grits. Makes 4 servings.

Seafood Gumbo

My mother-in-law was born in New Orleans and reared in Mobile, Alabama. Her elder relatives orally passed on many of their cultural traditions, from generation to generation. She frequently heard stories about how the African-Creole cooks transformed the kitchens in Southern Louisiana, enriching dishes with a variety of new flavors and cooking techniques. Gumbo was one of the dishes that her relatives believed originated in the African-Creole kitchen.

Many cooks thicken this one-pot dish with flour and okra. Other cooks use file powder. File powder is a spice, made from the dried, ground leaves of the sassafras tree. It can be used as a thickener or serve purely as a seasoning. Although file seasoning is readily available throughout New Orleans, I have only been able to purchase this seasoning at a few specialty food shops in New York. This is why I use okra and flour in my gumbo as a thickening agent.

New Orleans cooks also use tomatoes and other vegetables to enhance the flavor of gumbo. When I first began preparing gumbo, I asked my mother-in-law to serve as one of my tasters. I wanted to make certain that I had captured the essence of this dish. I now serve this dish in a cup as an appetizer or over rice as an entree. For a different flavor, I occasionally use ham or chicken in place of seafood.

8 oz. unsalted butter
1 cup all-purpose flour
2 medium onions, chopped
1 medium green pepper, chopped
1 14½-oz. can stewed tomatoes
½ lb. fresh okra, cut in small disks
1½ qt. chicken stock
8 oz. clam juice
2 tsp. chopped fresh garlic
2 lb. medium size shrimp, peeled and deveined
1 lb. lump crabmeat (or crab claw meat), picked over to remove cartilage
Salt and black pepper to taste
1 bunch chopped scallions
2 tbsp. chopped fresh parsley

Over medium heat, melt butter in a 4- or 5-quart pot. Add flour, stirring constantly until roux is dark brown. Add onions, green pepper, stewed tomatoes, and okra. Continue to cook for approximately five minutes. Add chicken stock and clam juice. Add garlic, shrimp, and crabmeat. Cover pot and reduce heat to a simmer. Continue to cook for approximately 20 minutes. Add salt and pepper to taste. Garnish with scallions and chopped parsley. Makes 12 servings.

Smothered Shrimp and Oysters

8 oz. unsalted butter
1 green pepper, finely chopped
1 small yellow onion, finely diced
8 oz. sliced button mushrooms
¼ cup chopped scallions
1 tsp. minced garlic
4 oz. all-purpose flour
2 cups shrimp or clam broth, hot
¼ cup heavy cream, hot
1 tsp. chopped pimento
20 large shrimp, peeled, deveined, and washed
½ lb. of oysters, in liquid
4 oz. sherry
Salt and pepper to taste

Melt butter in a large saucepan on medium heat. Add peppers, onions, mushrooms, scallions, and garlic. Sauté for approximately 3 minutes. Slowly stir in flour and cook an additional 2 minutes. Add hot broth and milk gradually to keep consistency of sauce smooth. Stir in pimento, salt, and pepper. Add sherry to sauce and stir in gently. Add shrimp and oysters with liquid. Simmer for 6 minutes. Serve hot over white rice or grits. Makes 8 servings.

Smothered Shrimp and Scallops

4 oz. vegetable oil
4 oz. all-purpose flour
1 medium onion, cut in strips
1 medium green pepper, cut in strips
½ cup sliced mushrooms
Salt to taste
Cayenne pepper to taste
12 medium shrimp peeled, deveined, and washed
8 large scallops
2 cups chicken stock, hot

Combine oil and flour together in a medium saucepan to form a roux. Cook roux over low heat, stirring occasionally with a wooden spoon. Cook very slowly until the roux becomes light brown. Add onions, peppers, and mushrooms. Season with salt and cayenne pepper. Continue to stir and add shrimp, scallops, and chicken stock. Stir until seafood is mixed well. Cover pan and cook for about 10 minutes or until scallops turn opaque and shrimp turns pink. Serve hot over white rice. Makes 4 servings.

Shrimp and Chicken Étouffée

I am so fortunate to have family members who live in Mobile, Alabama and in New Orleans. Whenever I visit my mother-in-law in Mobile, we always visit her relatives in New Orleans. Although one of my culinary arts instructors introduced me to this dish, I always look forward to sampling different chefs' variations of this dish when I am in New Orleans.

Étouffée is another standard dish in Southern Louisiana. Southerners love seasoned food and this is a very flavorful dish. Although some of my customers have difficulty pronouncing étouffée, it does not keep them from ordering this dish. The well-browned roux is what gives this dish a beautiful mahogany hue. My customers frequently request this dish when I offer it as one of the choices on the "Chef's Specials" menu.

2 strips bacon, diced
2 oz. chopped onions
2 tsp. all-purpose flour
½ cup chicken stock
4 oz. chicken cutlets, cubed
½ lb. shrimp, peeled, deveined, and washed
Chopped fresh garlic to taste
Salt and pepper to taste

Place a saucepan on medium heat. Once the pan is hot, add diced bacon and cook until crispy. Remove bacon from pan and set aside. Add onions to bacon drippings. Cook onions approximately 2 minutes. Slowly stir 2 teaspoons of flour into saucepan with onions and bacon drippings. Cook until flour is brown. Make certain not to burn flour. Whisk chicken stock into mixture in saucepan. Add chicken to mixture. Cover and cook approximately 2 minutes. Remove cover and add shrimp, garlic, and cooked bacon. Cook an additional 3 to 4 minutes. Add salt and pepper to taste. Serve immediately over grits or rice. Makes 4 servings.

Crabmeat Dumplings

¼ lb. unsalted butter
½ cup minced onions
½ cup milk
4 large eggs
2½ cups all-purpose flour
2 tsp. baking powder
¼ tsp. salt
1 tsp. Seafood seasoning seasoning
¼ tsp. black pepper
1 tbsp. Dijon mustard
2 tbsp. mayonnaise
2 cups crab meat, all shells and cartilage removed

Combine all dry ingredients in a medium bowl. Set aside. Using low heat, melt butter in a medium saucepan. Add minced onions. Cook onions for approximately 2 minutes until onions are tender. Do not brown onions. Remove saucepan from heat. Add milk, mustard, and mayonnaise to saucepan (still removed from heat). Mix ingredients well. Add eggs and beat for about two minutes. Add mixture to dry ingredients. Mix well. Fold in crabmeat. Mixture should resemble consistency of mashed potatoes. To cook the dumplings, using a teaspoon, drop batter into a rack in a steamer. Steam dumplings until cooked, approximately 8 to 10 minutes. Makes 8 servings.

Crab Cakes with Sliced Okra

1 lb. backfin crab meat
1 cup sliced okra
2 tsp. chopped fresh parsley
3 slices of white bread, crust removed and broken up in small pieces
½ cup mayonnaise
¼ cup Dijon mustard
1 tsp. Seafood seasoning seasoning
2 tsp. Worcestershire sauce
½ tsp. cayenne pepper
2 tsp. fresh lemon juice
2 large eggs
1 cup canola oil

Preheat oven to 350 degrees. In medium bowl, mix all ingredients together except the canola oil. Shape mixture into 4-oz. patties. Pour canola oil in medium-sized frying pan on medium heat (approximately 325 degrees). Place patties in frying pan and cook for 2 minutes on each side or until patties are brown. Once patties are browned, place them on a medium-sized sheet pan. Finish in the oven for about 8 minutes. Makes 8 servings.

Southern Fried Whiting

I always sell whiting fillets, carefully considering the well-being of my customers. I prefer fresh fish because the taste is far superior to frozen. Deep-frying is definitely the most popular method that my customers request for me to prepare this fish. Customers can also select to have their whiting broiled, barbecued, blackened, or fried. I have to admit, when properly seasoned and battered, fried fish with a wedge of lemon, a dollop of tartar sauce, and a side of coleslaw, easily lulls me into a blissful state of mind.

 8 pieces whiting, fillet
 Salt and pepper to taste
 1 tsp. seafood seasoning
 1 cup buttermilk
 1 cup milk
 2 large eggs
 1 lb. all-purpose flour
 1 lb. yellow cornmeal
 3 cups canola oil
 4 lemon wedges, for garnish

Rinse whiting in cold water. Pat dry with paper towel. Season fish with salt, pepper, and seafood seasoning. Set aside. Combine buttermilk, milk, and eggs in a medium bowl, creating an egg wash. Beat ingredients well. Set aside. Dredge fish in flour and shake off excess flour. Dip fish in egg wash and then in cornmeal. Set aside.

Heat oil in iron skillet to approximately 350 degrees. Pan fry fish in hot oil until golden brown. Drain oil from fish on paper towel. Garnish with lemon wedge. Makes 4 servings.

Deep-Fried Red Snapper Topped with Stewed Tomatoes and Baby Clams

Tomatoes add flavor to any dish. However, they have an unusually large amount of water. Stewing requires simmering food in a small amount of liquid, which generally creates a sauce to serve. To minimize the excess liquid in the tomatoes, cut the tomatoes in half and carefully squeeze out the seeds and most of the fluid. Although I fry the fish without flour or cornmeal, the snapper retains its moisture and the texture of its surface is crispy.

> 4-1 lb. red snapper
> Seafood seasoning to taste
> Salt and black pepper to taste
> 2 tbsp. olive oil, for sautéing vegetables and clams
> 2 tbsp. chopped onion
> 2 tbsp. chopped green pepper
> 1 tbsp. minced garlic
> 1 tbsp. sugar
> 1 14½-oz. can stewed tomatoes
> 1 small can whole baby clams
> 4 cups vegetable oil, for frying fish

Season fish with seafood seasoning, salt, and pepper. Set aside and begin preparing stewed tomatoes with baby clam sauce.

Pour olive oil in medium saucepan on low heat and add onions, green pepper, garlic, pepper, sugar, tomatoes, and clams. Cook tomato mixture for 15 minutes. Simmer on low heat while frying snapper.

To fry the snapper, place vegetable oil in a large cast-iron frying pan. Heat oil to 350 degrees. Place fish in hot oil and fry 10 minutes on each side. Remove fish from oil and drain on paper towel. Serve fish topped with stewed tomatoes and clam sauce. Makes 4 servings.

Spicy Whole Red Snapper

This dish is somewhat suggestive of a Jamaican dish. Jerk seasoning is a traditional blend of spices that gives food a very pungent taste. I have never visited Jamaica. However, many of my Caribbean customers repeatedly reassure me that I have definitely captured the taste of their cuisine.

½ cup fish sauce
Juice from 1 lime
2 tbsp. chili sauce
2 tbsp. minced fresh garlic
1 tbsp. grated fresh ginger
1 tbsp. jerk seasoning
1 tbsp. chopped fresh cilantro
2 tbsp. chopped scallions
2 cups coconut milk
Salt and black pepper to taste
2 lb. whole red snapper, with head intact,
   cleaned and scaled

Preheat oven to 325 degrees. In a medium bowl, combine all ingredients except the salt, pepper, and fish. Mix ingredients well. Set aside.

Place aluminum foil in the bottom of a shallow baking dish. Season snapper with salt and pepper. Place the snapper on top of foil in baking dish and gather foil around fish to resemble a boat. Pour mixture over fish and bake in the oven for 25 to 35 minutes or until fish flakes when tested with fork. Serve hot. Makes 4 servings.

Whole Baked Red Snapper Stuffed with Spinach

If you want to create an elegant savory indulgence for your guests, serve this dish. For your convenience, ask your fish monger to remove the bones.

> 8 oz. olive oil
> 1 bunch California spinach, washed, cleaned, and stems removed
> 1 lb. sliced button mushrooms
> 1 medium onion, diced small
> 1 cup plain breadcrumbs
> 1 tsp. minced fresh garlic
> Salt and black pepper to taste
> 4 1-lb. whole red snappers
> 4 oz. unsalted butter

Place olive oil in a medium pot. Add onions, mushrooms, spinach, and garlic. Cook 5 minutes. Add breadcrumbs. Season with salt and pepper to taste. Cook for an additional 5 minutes. Remove from heat and set aside until ready to stuff snapper.

Divide spinach mixture into four equal parts. Stuff each cavity of the fish with spinach mixture. Place stuffed fish in shallow baking dish. Season with salt and pepper and top with butter. Bake fish in 350-degree oven for 20 to 25 minutes or until fish flakes when tested with fork. Serve hot, with or without yogurt sauce. Makes 4 servings.

Lobster Stuffed with Mashed Potatoes

Mashed potatoes are a surefire comfort food. Dressing up even the most basic comfort food can make a memorable meal. This has served as a splendid choice for an elegant dinner because of the way I present this entree. Maine lobster is available almost anywhere. I prepared this dish during one of my appearances on a television network show devoted to teaching viewers cooking techniques. The producer entitled this show A Romantic Dinner for Two. *This dish has become a favorite on the special menu that I offer on Valentine's Day. I always prepare the mashed potatoes prior to getting the lobster ready for stuffing.*

2 medium Russet potatoes
4 oz. melted unsalted butter, for potatoes
½ cup heavy cream
2 tbsp. sour cream
1 tsp. chopped scallions
1 tsp. salt, for potatoes
½ tsp. black pepper, for potatoes
1½ qt. water, for boiling potatoes
2 live 1½ pound lobsters
Salt and pepper to taste
6 oz. melted unsalted butter
2 tbsp. lemon juice
1 cup water
2 lemon wedges
2 wooden skewers, soaked in cold water

Dice potatoes into 1-inch cubes. Place 1½ quarts of water in medium pot over high heat. When the water boils, add the potatoes. Cover the potatoes and cook until fork tender. When potatoes are cooked, drain well using a colander. While the potatoes are draining in colander, melt butter in small pot. Add heavy cream to butter. Bring butter and cream to a boil. Remove from stove. Place drained potatoes in a mixing bowl. Set electric mixer to medium speed and begin whipping potatoes. With machine running, slowly add heavy cream and butter. Whip potatoes until smooth (approximately 4 to 5 minutes). Stop machine and remove bowl. Fold in sour cream and scallions. Add salt and pepper. Set aside.

Wash live lobsters under cold water, leaving rubber bands on claws. To kill a lobster, sever its spinal cord (the method least painful for the lobster). Deaden its sense of pain by thrusting the tip of the knife between the lobster's eyes and continue moving downward into the natural breach where the head and front abdomen shell meet. Turn lobster around and split down the tail, but do not cut in half. Discard stomach. Remove rubber bands from claws. Place lobsters on baking dish or baking pan. Insert wooden skewers through the length of tails. Season with salt, pepper, and 2 ounces of butter.

Place a star tip on pastry bag. Place mashed potatoes in pastry bag. Pipe mashed potatoes into front cavity of lobster and bake in 375-degree oven for approximately 15 minutes. Serve lobster with melted butter and lemon wedges. Makes 2 servings.

Poultry, Meats, and Game

Chicken is a mainstay of Southern fare as well as in most kitchens throughout the world. Practically all supermarkets maintain an abundance of excellent quality chickens that are inexpensive, low in fat, and suitable for most styles of entertaining. Everyone seems to enjoy chicken prepared some kind of way, but reflecting back on childhood memories, it is a wonder that I still eat chicken. There are two experiences that I will never forget.

The first experience that should have ended my love for chicken was when I first saw my Aunt Edna wring a chicken's neck. She then dipped the chicken into boiling hot water and proceeded to pluck its feathers. I was horrified. I did not know that this practice was common throughout the south. I just thought it was another one of Aunt Edna's antics. Aunt Edna was a fierce individual who did not back down from any challenge. Needless to say, I made a point of staying on her good side, though I would not eat chicken for months after watching Aunt Edna slay her chicken.

My second experience was years later when I was approximately twelve years old. This particular afternoon, my parents were at church attending a special program. My twin sister and I decided that we did not want the meal that my mother had prepared for us to eat. We wanted to eat fried chicken. On numerous occasions we had watched both of our parents fry chicken, so we were certain that we could prepare this dish with ease. We busily went about the routine of gathering all our ingredients.

Our first mistake was that we chose a hen rather than a fryer. For those novices who do not know the difference, it is better to bake or roast a hen because of the size and age of the bird. A fryer is a younger chicken and weighs approximately 2 to 3 pounds. The meat of a fryer is much tenderer than that of a hen, which makes it much more appropriate for frying.

Nonetheless, my sister and I proceeded to fry the hen. We anxiously waited for the hen to cook; it seemed to take longer than we expected. We thought the time factor was because we were so eager to eat. Finally, after waiting for what seemed a lifetime, we removed the chicken from the pan. My sister and I were extremely disappointed upon taking our first bite. The chicken was as tough as leather.

Of course we did not want our parents to know that we had cooked without their supervision, so we tried to discard the chicken in our backyard. As luck would have it, we saw our parents returning home much earlier that we anticipated. As we scurried, trying to grab up all of the cooking ingredients, I accidentally tipped the frying pan containing the hot oil on my leg. I knew that I had burnt my leg badly. However, I grew up during the time in which folks believed in the Bible verse that adults frequently quoted, "Spare the rod and spoil the child." In that moment, I thought it best to bear the pain of the burn, rather than the potential pain of my mother's "rod."

Although I tried to care for my wound, I was in pain the entire night.
The next day, I awoke with a blister on my leg. Frightened half to death, I felt I had no other choice but to tell my mother about my burn.

My mother was upset, but at that moment I think she realized how fearful I was of her chastisements. She took me to the doctor and upon returning home made me promise that regardless of whatever happened, if I injured myself, I must always let her know.

When my customers tell me that I fry the best chicken that they have ever eaten, I thank them for the compliment and then smile, thinking to myself, "If they only knew."

I sell more fried chicken than any other item on the menu. Although there are several restaurants that specialize in serving Southern cuisine, I am the only chef who has won a Golden Dish award from *Gentleman's Quarterly* magazine for the best fried chicken and waffles. I included my award-winning recipe for fried chicken in this chapter along with other recipes for meat and game.

Baked Chicken with Herb Vinaigrette Dressing

½ cup balsamic vinegar
¼ cup red wine vinegar
1 tbsp. Dijon mustard
¼ cup chopped fresh basil
2 tbsp. chopped fresh garlic
1 tbsp. fresh tarragon
1 tbsp. red chili paste
¾ cup olive oil
1 3-lb. chicken, cut into 8 pieces
Salt and black pepper to taste

Preheat oven to 350 degrees. In a blender or food processor, combine the first 7 ingredients on slow speed for 3 minutes. Add the olive oil and blend for an additional 3 minutes. Remove vinaigrette from blender or food processor and refrigerate until ready to use.

Wash chicken under cold water. Pat dry with paper towel and season with salt and pepper. Place chicken pieces on a 9 x 13 baking sheet, skin side up. Pour vinaigrette over chicken, cover, and refrigerate 2 hours, turning every 30 minutes.

Cover and bake chicken for 35 minutes. Remove cover from chicken and bake uncovered for an additional 30 minutes until skin is crispy and the juices from the chicken run clear. Serve hot over braised kale (see index). Makes 4 servings.

Baked Peach Rum Chicken

1 3-lb. chicken, cut into 8 pieces
Salt to taste
White pepper to taste
4 oz. unsalted butter
1 tbsp. light brown sugar
8 oz. orange juice
4 oz. dark rum
1 tsp. fresh grated ginger
8 oz. peach nectar
2 peaches, cut into quarters and pits removed

Preheat oven to 325 degrees. Season chicken with salt and pepper and set aside.

In a heavy medium pot combine the butter, sugar, orange juice, rum, grated ginger, and peach nectar. Cook peach and rum mixture for 5 minutes on low heat until sugar dissolves. Remove pot from heat.

Place chicken in a medium baking dish, skin side up. Pour peach and rum mixture over chicken. Cover and bake for approximately 40 minutes. Remove chicken from oven and uncover. Top with peach quarters. Baste chicken with sauce and return to oven uncovered. Bake for 2 additional minutes. Makes 4 servings.

Chicken and Dumplings

My father often made chicken and dumplings for Sunday dinner. I enjoyed this dish, but his dumplings were heavy and caused everyone to be sluggish. Anyone who ate his dumplings always wanted to take a nap at the end of the meal.

My dumplings are much more refined than typical dumplings. I use eggs, whereas many cooks only use shortening and flour. Adding a variety of vegetables provides additional color and taste. Finally, I steam my dumplings as opposed to boiling, which also makes them lighter.

I prepare this dish in three simple stages. The recipe may seem a little involved at first sight, but the outcome is worth the time it takes to prepare this amazing dish. Much to the dismay of my staff, I never have leftovers of this dish, regardless of the amount I make.

1 3 to 3½ lb. chicken
1 tsp. salt
1 tsp. black pepper
4 oz. vegetable oil
½ cup chopped onion
½ cup chopped celery
½ cup chopped carrots
½ cup sliced mushrooms
1 bay leaf
48 oz. chicken stock
4 oz. melted unsalted butter
4 oz. flour
¼ cup chopped fresh parsley

Preheat oven to 375 degrees. Cut chicken into 8 pieces. Wash chicken, removing all visible fat, then season chicken with salt and pepper.

Heat vegetable oil in roasting pan on top of stove. Place chicken in heated vegetable oil and brown chicken on both sides. Add vegetables and bay leaf. Sauté vegetables 1 minute. Add chicken stock. Cover roasting pan and place chicken in oven. Prepare the dumplings while the chicken is baking. Bake chicken for 30 minutes or until chicken is done. Remove chicken from oven.

To create the sauce, remove chicken and vegetables from roasting pan. Leaving chicken stock in pan, place roasting pan on top of stove over low heat. Place small saucepan on low heat and pour melted butter into saucepan. Stir the flour into the melted butter for approximately 3 minutes, creating a roux. Whisk roux into chicken stock, creating a sauce. Once sauce has thickened, put chicken and vegetables back into roasting pan.

Add cooked dumplings and simmer for approximately 4 minutes before serving. Garnish with chopped parsley. Makes 4 servings.

Dumplings

¼ lb. melted butter
½ cup minced onions
½ cup milk
4 eggs
2 tsp. baking powder
¼ tsp. black pepper
¼ tsp. salt
2½ cups all-purpose flour

Using low heat, melt butter in medium saucepan. Add minced onions and cook for approximately 2 minutes or until onions are tender. Do not brown onions. Remove saucepan from heat. Pour onions and butter into a medium bowl. Add milk and eggs. Mix well. Add all dry ingredients to the milk and egg mixture. Mix ingredients well. Mixture should resemble consistency of mashed potatoes.

Using a teaspoon, drop the batter onto a rack in a steamer. Steam until dumplings are cooked, approximately 4 to 6 minutes. Makes 4 servings.

Oatmeal Pancakes Stuffed with Chicken Strips, Topped with Pecan Syrup

This is a delightful dish that is fantastic throughout the day and is great for late-night munchies. Taking the extra step to prepare the pecan syrup will create pure ecstasy.

For the Chicken Strips

4 chicken cutlets
Salt and pepper to taste
1 lb. all-purpose flour
2 cups canola oil

Cut each chicken cutlet into 3 strips and season with salt and pepper. Dredge the chicken in flour and shake off excess.

Pour oil into heavy iron skillet and heat over medium-high heat. Place chicken strips into hot oil. Fry chicken until bottom is golden brown. Using tongs, turn the chicken and brown on other side. Lower the heat if necessary to avoid burning. Continue to cook the chicken for approximately 5 to 7 minutes, turning once or twice until fully cooked. Remove chicken from pan and drain well on paper towels. Makes 4 servings.

For the Oatmeal Pancakes

1½ cups self rising flour
1 tsp. baking powder
1 cup old-fashioned oats
1 tsp. baking soda
4 tbsp. sugar
1 tsp. salt
3 cups buttermilk
2 large eggs
1 tsp. vanilla extract
4 oz. melted sweet butter
3 oz. canola oil to grease griddle

In a medium bowl, mix all dry ingredients together. Set aside. In a medium bowl combine buttermilk, eggs, and vanilla extract. Using a wire whip, whisk ingredients together for approximately 1 minute. Add dry ingredients to buttermilk mixture. Add melted butter and continue to mix until batter is fairly smooth. Allow pancake mixture to rest for 10 minutes before cooking.

For each pancake, pour approximately ¼ cup batter onto lightly-greased griddle. Turn pancake when edges look brown and bubbles appear on top. Turn each pancake one time. Remove pancakes from griddle.

To stuff pancakes, place each pancake on a plate. Place one chicken strip on edge of each pancake and roll each pancake until thoroughly wrapped around chicken strip. Place crease down on plate. Use pecan syrup recipe for added treat. Makes 4 servings.

For the Pecan Syrup

8 oz. melted sweet butter
1 cup pecans
16 oz. maple syrup

Place melted butter in a medium saucepan over medium heat. Add pecans and maple syrup. Stir mixture. Simmer for approximately 5 minutes or until syrup is hot. Spoon over stuffed pancakes. Makes 4 servings.

Coq Au Vin

This is an impressive and elegant dish that is easily prepared with little fuss.

2 tbsp. oil
2 tbsp. butter
3 oz. diced lean bacon
½ onion, julienne
1½ lb. chicken cutlets, cut in cubes
1 tbsp. all-purpose flour
1 cup warm chicken stock
1 cup red wine
¼ cup julienne carrots
½ cup sliced mushroom
1 sprig rosemary
1 tbsp. chopped parsley

Heat oil and butter in a heavy pan. Add bacon and onions. Cook until golden brown. Remove the bacon and onions from pan. Set aside.

Place chicken in pan and cook in drippings approximately 3 minutes. Remove chicken from pan. Set aside.

Sprinkle flour in pan and cook in drippings approximately 2 minutes, stirring well. Add warm chicken stock. Stir well, creating a gravy. Return chicken, bacon, and onions to pan. Pour in wine. Cover and simmer for 5 minutes. Add carrots, mushrooms, and rosemary. Simmer for an additional 7 minutes. Sprinkle with parsley and serve. Makes 4 servings.

Fried Chicken

2 cups buttermilk
2 tbsp. hot sauce
2 tbsp. kosher salt
2 3-lb. chickens, each cut into 8 pieces
2 cups all-purpose flour
2 tsp. baking powder
1 tsp. ground black pepper
1 tsp. garlic powder
½ tsp. paprika
5 cups canola oil, for frying

In a large plastic freezer bag, combine buttermilk, hot sauce, and 1 tbsp. kosher salt. Add pieces of chicken, turning to coat thoroughly. Seal bag, pressing out air. Place bag in refrigerator and marinate for 3 hours.

In a medium bowl, stir flour, baking powder, pepper, garlic powder, paprika, and remaining tablespoon of salt until well mixed. When the marinating process is complete, pour oil in a heavy gauge frying pan. Heat oil to 325 degrees. Place chicken in oil skin side down, 4 pieces at a time. Fry chicken 12 minutes on each side. Repeat this step for the remaining 4 pieces of chicken. Drain chicken on paper towel. Serve hot or at room temperature. Makes 4 servings.

Southern Fried Chicken

It is so true that there are as many recipes for fried chicken as there are cooks in the South. However, I am sure that we all agree on one thing—the secret to great fried chicken is to immerse fresh chicken completely in oil that has been heated to a high temperature. I only fry chicken in a cast-iron frying pan because heavy metal helps to hold the oil at a constant temperature.

It is essential to maintain the oil at a very hot temperature at all times. Otherwise the chicken will absorb the oil, causing the chicken to become greasy. Also, don't overcrowd the pan. Overcrowding will cool the oil, and the chicken will not cook or brown evenly. When a piece of chicken starts to float a little in the oil, it is done. I strongly encourage cooks to try fried chicken with a waffle. Do not forget to use maple syrup or your favorite topping.

1 2½- to 3-lb. chicken
Salt and pepper to taste
Garlic powder to taste
1 lb. flour
2 cups oil

Cut chicken into 8 pieces. Season chicken with salt, pepper, and garlic powder. Dredge the chicken in flour and shake off excess.

Pour oil into heavy iron skillet. Heat over medium-high heat for about 4 minutes. When the oil starts to bubble it is ready for frying. Place the chicken pieces skin side down in hot oil. Fry the chicken until golden brown on the bottom. Turn the pieces with tongs and brown on the other side. Lower the heat if necessary to avoid burning. Continue to cook the chicken, turning once or twice. Cook 20 to 30 minutes, depending on size of chicken and temperature of oil. Remove chicken from pan and drain well on paper towels. Serve hot or cold. Makes 4 servings.

Marinated Chicken Wings

½ cup Teriyaki sauce
2 tbsp. Dijon mustard
2 tbsp. honey
2 tsp. grated fresh ginger
2 tsp. minced fresh garlic
12 chicken wings

Preheat oven to 325 degrees. Combine all ingredients except chicken in a non-metal medium bowl. Mix well. Place chicken wings in marinade and coat well. Cover chicken and refrigerate overnight.

Remove chicken from refrigerator and place in a shallow pan lined with aluminum foil. Place uncovered chicken in oven on the middle rack and cook for 25 minutes. After 25 minutes, turn chicken wings and raise the temperature to 375 degrees. Cook for an additional 15 minutes. Remove chicken wings from oven and serve hot with or without spicy mayonnaise. Makes 4 servings.

Spicy Mayonnaise

1 cup mayonnaise
1 tsp. cayenne pepper
1 tbsp. hot sauce

Combine all ingredients in a small bowl. Mix well. Refrigerate until ready to use. Makes 4 servings.

Lemon-Marinated Filet Mignon

4 to 6-lb. filet, trimmed and tied by butcher
1 tsp. grated lemon
Juice from 1 lemon
8 oz. olive oil
1 chopped small bunch of scallions
4 tsp. sugar
3 tsp. salt
2 tbsp. Worcestershire sauce
1 tsp. Dijon mustard
1 tbsp. cracked black pepper
2 oz. walnut oil

Place beef in a shallow baking dish. Set aside. In a mixing bowl combine the remaining ingredients except the walnut oil. Mix well and pour mixture over beef. Refrigerate 1 hour. Turn beef every 20 minutes within the hour. Remove beef from marinade, reserving marinade in refrigerator. Pat beef dry with paper towel. Set aside.

Preheat oven to 400 degrees. Place a large cast-iron skillet with grill marks on stove over high heat. Wait 5 minutes until skillet is hot. Brush beef with walnut oil and place meat in hot skillet. Turn every 4 minutes until both sides are brown.

Remove skillet from stove and place in oven for 12 minutes. Remove beef from oven and place on serving platter. Allow meat to rest for approximately 10 minutes. Place remaining marinade in a small pot and bring to a boil. Spoon marinade over meat. Makes 8 servings.

Baked Ham

    1 10-lb. ham, bone in
    2 qt. cold water
    2 cups crushed pineapples
    1 tsp. ground cloves
    ¼ lb. dark brown sugar

Preheat oven to 325 degrees. In a large pot, boil ham in 2 quarts of cold water over medium heat for 1 hour. Remove ham from boiling water and place the ham fat side up in a roasting pan. Score top of ham with X-shaped cuts. Set aside.

Combine pineapple, cloves, and sugar. Mix well. Coat the ham with the mixture. Decrease temperature of the oven to 300 degrees and bake ham for 2 hours, basting every 30 minutes. Cool ham. Slice and serve with side dishes, salads, mini corn muffins, or on a buffet. Makes 12 servings.

Grilled Marinated Lamb Chops

    8 lamb chops
    Kosher salt to taste
    Black pepper to taste
    1 cup extra virgin olive oil
    3 tsp. balsamic vinegar
    1 tbsp. Dijon mustard
    1 tbsp. chopped fresh garlic
    2 tbsp. chopped fresh rosemary

Season each lamb chop with salt and pepper. Set aside. In a medium bowl, whisk remaining ingredients. Place lamb chops in heavy-duty freezer bag. Pour marinade in bag over lamb chops, making sure lamb chops are coated with marinade. Allow lamb chops to marinate for at least 30 minutes before grilling.

Heat cast-iron skillet with grill marks until skillet is very hot. Remove lamb chops from marinade and pat semi dry. Place lamb chops on hot skillet and cook to desired temperature or approximately 3 minutes on each side. Makes 4 servings.

Meat Loaf

When I first opened the restaurant, meat loaf was not on the menu. I guess this entree did not particularly excite me. However, as customers began developing personal relationships with me, they began requesting some of their favorite dishes. Periodically, someone would request meat loaf. I underestimated how fond customers were of this dish, and I dragged my heels fulfilling their requests.

Fortunately, one of my customers was extremely persistent. He even resorted to asking my wife to whisper the word "meat loaf" in my ear at night as I was falling asleep. Finally, this gentleman, who is a minister, told my wife that he had talked to God about the matter. The minister assured my wife that if I put meat loaf on the menu, it would become a big seller.

After that conversation, my wife suggested that I prepare meat loaf as a daily special and test the market. Meat loaf topped with brown gravy is now one of my best sellers. The persistent minister, who I now affectionately call "Meat Loaf," always reminds me that he was the one who influenced me to expand my menu. Many of my customers claim that they have never had meat loaf that tastes as good as mine. I hope every cook who tries this recipe gets the same reaction.

2 lb. ground chuck
1 lb. ground sirloin
1 tbsp. finely chopped green pepper
2 tbsp. minced onions
2 tbsp. Worcestershire sauce
1 tsp. minced fresh garlic
¼ cup catsup
¼ cup milk
¼ cup plain breadcrumbs
3 large eggs, beaten
1½ tsp. kosher salt
1 tsp. black pepper
1 tsp. onion pepper
2 cups water

Preheat oven to 350 degrees. In a large bowl mix well all ingredients except water. Place 1½ feet of heavy duty foil in a loaf pan. Put a piece of 1-foot parchment paper on top of foil. Fold the parchment and foil paper into the shape of the loaf pan. Spread meat loaf mixture the length of the parchment paper. Fold the parchment and foil paper into the shape of the loaf pan Fold the top and bottom first and then the sides of the paper. Pour water into the bottom of the loaf pan. Bake in oven for 1 hour and 10 minutes or until the internal temperature of the loaf is 160 degrees. Serve hot. Makes 8 servings.

Oxtail Ragout

This delicious family-style stew is a hearty way to serve oxtails. When served over rice, this ragout makes a welcome main dish.

- 2 lb. oxtails, cut into 2-inch pieces with fat trimmed off
- Salt and pepper to taste
- ½ cup flour
- 2 tbsp. olive oil
- 2 tbsp. unsalted butter
- 2 cups dry red wine
- 3 cups beef broth
- 1 medium onion, chopped small
- ¼ cup finely chopped celery
- ¼ cup baby carrots
- 1 cup button mushrooms, cut in halves
- 1 tsp. minced fresh garlic
- 2 bay leaves
- 3 sprigs thyme
- 1 tsp. chopped fresh rosemary
- 4 small red potatoes, cut in halves
- 1 tsp. sugar

Preheat oven to 300 degrees. Season oxtails with salt and pepper. Dredge oxtails in flour and set aside. Heat oil and butter in Dutch oven or large skillet with tight-fitting lid. Place oxtails in Dutch oven or skillet on medium-high heat. Stir frequently for approximately 10 minutes or until oxtails are well browned.

Turn heat down and add wine, broth, onions, and celery. Cover with lid and place in oven. Cook for two hours.

Remove from oven and uncover. Add carrots, mushrooms, garlic, bay leaves, thyme, rosemary, potatoes, and sugar. Cover and cook in oven for an additional 40 minutes or until oxtails are tender. Remove from oven and serve hot with white rice. Makes 6 servings.

Barbecue Baby Back Ribs

One of the wonderful aspects that I enjoy about operating a restaurant is that I have had the opportunity to develop new friendships. When I initially opened the restaurant, I would tell everyone whom I encountered about Richard's Place. One person I met was a bachelor who worked for one of the local police precincts. Each evening after work he would stop in the restaurant for dinner. He has been eating at the restaurant ever since. Jeff has become a very close friend of mine, and I have also become somewhat of his personal chef. It is not unusual for Jeff to call the restaurant in advance and ask me to prepare special dishes for him.

Jeff also has a special table where he typically sits, which is neatly tucked in a corner. One day while he was enjoying his baby back ribs, a little boy hurried past Jeff's table to reach the restroom. As the little boy passed Jeff's table, he suddenly stopped. He walked back to Jeff's table and asked if the ribs were really that good. Apparently, Jeff was passionately eating his ribs to the degree that he was oblivious to his surroundings. Jeff had to laugh at himself as he looked up from his plate and informed the little boy that the ribs were extremely good. When the little boy returned to his table, he ordered the baby back ribs. Jeff and I still joke about the manner in which he must have been eating the ribs to capture this little boy's attention.

4 slabs of baby back ribs
3 tbsp. paprika
1½ tbsp. light brown sugar
2¼ tsp. kosher salt
2 tsp. chili powder
1¼ tsp. ground cumin
¼ tsp. cayenne pepper
1 tsp. garlic powder
1 tsp. onion powder
3 cups ketchup
1 cup apple juice
¼ cup Worcestershire sauce
2 tbsp. brown sugar
2 tbsp. cider vinegar
3 tbsp. yellow mustard
1 tsp. ground black pepper
1 tbsp. white vinegar

In a small bowl, combine paprika, light brown sugar, salt, chili powder, ground cumin, cayenne pepper, garlic powder, and onion powder. Mix well. Season ribs on both sides with spice mixture. Cover ribs and bake at 300 degrees for 1 hour and 15 minutes.

Immediately after placing ribs in oven, begin preparing the barbecue sauce. In a medium pot on low heat, combine remaining ingredients to create the sauce. Allow sauce to simmer for 1 hour. Uncover ribs after cooking for the allotted time and baste both sides with barbecue sauce. Cook ribs an additional 45 minutes. Makes 4 servings.

Pan-Grilled Beer-Marinated Pork Chops

4 8-oz. center cut pork chops
1 bottle dark beer
Salt and pepper to taste
4 oz. melted unsalted butter
3 tbsp. fresh lemon juice
2 tbsp. olive oil

Place pork chops in a medium bowl. Pour beer over pork chops, coating well. Cover bowl and marinate pork chops in refrigerator for 1 hour.

Place a cast-iron frying pan with grill marks on medium heat. Remove pork chops from beer and drain briefly. Discard beer. Season pork chops with salt and pepper.

Combine butter, lemon juice, and olive oil in a small bowl. Coat each pork chop with butter mixture. Save remaining mixture for basting. Place pork chops into grill pan when it becomes hot. Turn pork chops as needed, basting several times with remaining butter mixture. Cook approximately 5 minutes on each side until pork chops are done. Serve hot. Makes 4 servings.

Grilled Boneless Pork Chops

To ensure that I serve tender and juicy pork chops, I always purchase center cuts, with or without the bone. Grilling is a wonderfully healthy alternative to frying pork chops. When served with my recipe for pear salsa, this dish is easy to add to any repertoire of menus.

    4 5-oz. boneless pork chops
    Salt and pepper to taste
    4 oz. olive oil

    Season pork chops with salt and pepper. Set aside until ready to grill.
    Place a cast-iron skillet with grill marks on medium heat. Coat skillet with oil. When oil is hot, place pork chops in skillet. Grill pork chops for 6 minutes on each side. Remove pork chops from skillet and serve with pear salsa (see index) and a tossed salad. Makes 4 servings.

Smothered Pork Chops

Even when I am entertaining at home, the familiar smell of sizzling pork chops always arouses my guests. They take turns coming into the kitchen, eagerly waiting for me to tell them that they will eat shortly. Smothering pork chops helps to permeate all the flavors throughout the pork chops. I love eating cheese grits and biscuits with smothered pork chops.

    1¼ cup vegetable oil, for frying
    4 6-oz. center cut pork chops, with bone
    Salt and pepper to taste
    1 cup flour
    4 cups warm chicken stock
    1 large onion, sliced
    1 tbsp. Gravy Master®

    Place a large cast-iron skillet on medium heat. Add vegetable oil. Season pork chops with salt and pepper, then dredge pork chops in flour. When oil is 325 degrees, place pork chops in skillet.

Cook pork chops on each side approximately 5 minutes. Remove pork chops from skillet and set aside.

Pour off fat from skillet leaving approximately 4 tbsp. oil. Do not scrape skillet. Return skillet to heat and add 4 tbsp. flour to drippings. Stir occasionally, allowing flour to brown. Add warm chicken stock. Whisk chicken stock and flour mixture carefully to prevent lumps. Return pork chops to skillet. Add onions and Gravy Master®. Cover skillet and simmer on low heat 25 to 30 minutes or until pork chops are tender. Makes 4 servings.

Barbecue Rib Eye Steak

1 tsp. minced garlic
2 sprigs of rosemary
1 cup olive oil
2 12-oz. rib eye steaks
2 oz. sweet butter
1 tbsp. grated Spanish onion
1 tsp. minced fresh garlic
¼ cup sugar
8 oz. Worcestershire sauce
1¼ cup ketchup
1 tsp. Dijon mustard
1 tsp. yellow mustard
½ tsp. jerk seasoning
1 tbsp. white vinegar
Salt and pepper to taste
Barbecue sauce to taste

Combine garlic, rosemary, and olive oil in a bowl. Place steaks in mixture and marinate for 1 hour before cooking. On low heat, melt butter in a small saucepan. Add grated onions, minced garlic, and sugar. Using a wooden spoon, stir mixture for approximately 3 minutes. Add remaining ingredients. Allow sauce to simmer 8 minutes, stirring occasionally.

Heat cast-iron skillet with grill marks until skillet is very hot. Remove steak from marinade and pat semi dry. Place steaks into hot skillet and cook to desired temperature. Baste steak with barbecue sauce to taste. Makes 2 servings.

Poultry, Meats, and Game

Rabbit and Shrimp Jambalaya

Rabbit is another food item that arouses mixed emotions when I reflect upon some of my childhood experiences. The first time I remember eating rabbit was after one of my father's hunting trips. I remember him preparing a rabbit stew that was absolutely delicious. I do not think I ever gave much thought to my father's role as a hunter when I was very young. All I knew was that rabbit stews appeared on our dining room table quite often. I recall periodically asking him if I could go hunting with him, but he always told me that I was not old enough.

One night, as he was cleaning his rifle and setting out his hunting attire, I asked him when was I going to be old enough to go hunting with him. Amazingly, he told me that if I got up early enough he would take me with him the following morning. I hardly slept that night.

I remember how excited I felt walking in the woods with my father. We talked and laughed until we reached the hunting area. Then he informed me that I would have to stop talking so that he could concentrate. I do not know what I expected, but the outing was an eye-opening experience. I remember quietly watching my father as he aimed his rifle and pulled the trigger. The sound echoed throughout the wooded area. My father told me to stay where I was standing while he went to retrieve the game. The sight of the dead rabbit nearly scared me to death. My father chuckled and asked me what did I think happened when he went hunting. I continued eating rabbit stew, but I never asked him to go hunting again.

Though rabbit meat has a delicate and pleasing taste, I do not get many requests to prepare rabbit dishes. On a few occasions, I have served rabbit stew on the Sunday dinner buffet. There was never one piece of rabbit left in the chafing dish. I am certain that everyone will love this dish. Domestic rabbit is readily available fresh or frozen in most parts of the U.S.

1 2- to 2½-lb. rabbit, cut in 8 to 10 pieces
Salt and pepper to taste
4 oz. olive oil
8 oz. finely chopped onions
8 oz. sliced mushrooms
8 oz. diced green pepper
4 oz. finely diced celery
1 tbsp. minced fresh garlic
1 4½-oz. can stewed tomatoes
1 bay leaf
1 lb. medium shrimp, peeled, cleaned, and deveined
2 cups raw long grain rice
2 cups heated chicken stock
2 tbsp. chopped fresh parsley

Season rabbit pieces with salt and pepper. Set aside.

Pour olive oil in a large, heave gauge pot on medium heat. Place rabbit in pot and cook on both sides approximately 14 minutes. Add onions, mushrooms, green pepper, celery, garlic, stewed tomatoes, and bay leaf. Cover pot and cook for 5 additional minutes.

Remove cover and add shrimp, rice, and chicken stock. Mix well and cover. Heat and simmer approximately 12 minutes or until rice is tender and shrimp are pink. Serve hot and garnish with chopped parsley. Makes 6 servings.

Side Dishes

SIDE DISHES

Collard greens, black-eyed peas, okra, sweet potatoes, corn, cabbage, tomatoes—the list seems endless. One thing I recall about living in the South is that if you knew how to plant vegetables, you would never be hungry. My parents grew cabbage, tomatoes, and potatoes that they often exchanged for other vegetables with neighbors and relatives who lived outside the city limits.

Along with providing nutrition, harvesting and preserving vegetables also seemed to create a reason for socializing. I recall times when one of my grandmothers would come to visit us from South Carolina, bringing watermelons that were in season. After we ate the meat of the watermelon, my mother would cook the rinds and create a jam that she preserved and we would later spread on home-baked bread. My mother also preserved peaches and pears and pickled tomatoes that she used at a later date. This preserving process often meant that my mother and other relatives would spend endless hours catching up on what was going on in other people's lives.

Some of the most memorable dinners were when my father returned from one of his hunting trips or fishing expeditions. He would stew whatever he caught with potatoes and tomatoes and a medley of seasonings.

When I recall my parents' method of preparing vegetables, I realize that they, too, were guilty of leaching the life and nutrients out of every vegetable they cooked. The green beans were always limp, the collard greens were cooked for hours, and the cabbage was lifeless. When I was a child, I hated the smell of cabbage. I often wondered why anyone wanted to eat anything that produced such an offensive odor as the cabbage that my mother cooked. As I embarked upon my own culinary experiences, I learned how to braise and sauté cabbage. These methods minimize the gaseous odors released when cooking cabbage.

When I first began serving green beans at my restaurant, many of my African-American customers would send back the beans that I always prepared *al dente*. I had many complaints that the beans were undercooked or too crispy. Some upset customers asked me why I did not thoroughly cook the green beans. They did not want "crunchy" green beans. Others offered to come into the kitchen to teach me how to cook green beans. Initially, I thought that I might have made a mistake trying to create healthy dishes. My wife spent many nights reassuring me that if I took the time to explain to the customers why I was not overcooking the vegetables, they would eventually appreciate my concern for their health. She was right. Now many of the same customers applaud me and tell other customers that I sure can cook vegetables.

I also roast vegetables. This method helps to seal in the juices and enhances the flavors. Grilling vegetables to use in salads has also become widely appreciated, especially amongst my vegetarian clientele. The dishes in this unit will add a finishing touch to most meat, fish, or poultry dishes. Many of the selections can stand alone, providing a healthy and flavorful dish for the vegetarian in any family.

Collard Greens with Smoked Turkey Wings

1 bunch collard greens
2 tbsp. vegetable oil
¾ cup minced onion
½ cup diced carrots
1 smoked turkey wing, cut in 4 pieces
2 gallons chicken stock
¼ balsamic vinegar
¼ cup brown sugar
¼ cup diced tomatoes

Cut collard greens, removing bottom stems up to the leaves. Stack 3 to 4 leaves. Roll leaves lengthwise and cut crossways in ½-inch strips. Continue process until all leaves are cut. Wash cut leaves thoroughly.

Pour vegetable oil into large heavy pot on medium heat. Once oil is hot, add ½ cup minced onions, ½ cup carrots, and all 4 pieces of smoked turkey. Sauté approximately 2 minutes. Add washed collard greens and chicken stock.

Cover pot and cook for approximately 1 hour and 45 minutes, or until greens are tender. Periodically check pot to make certain that stock does not evaporate. Add additional stock or water if needed. Once greens are tender, remove pot from stove.

Add vinegar and sugar to collard greens. Stir greens. Let greens stand for 2 minutes before serving. Garnish with remaining onions and diced tomatoes. Makes 6 servings.

Collard Greens and Turnip Greens with Smoked Ham Hocks and Smoked Neck Bones

1 bunch collard greens
2 bunches turnip greens
4 tbsp. olive oil
1 medium onion, finely chopped
1 cup finely chopped carrots
1 large red pepper, finely chopped
1 tbsp. finely chopped garlic
3 qt. chicken stock
1 small smoked ham hock
2 small smoked neck bones
1 cup apple cider vinegar
1/4 tsp. crushed red pepper flakes
2 tbsp. brown sugar

Cut collard greens and turnip greens, removing bottom stems up to the leaves. Stack 3 to 4 leaves. Roll leaves and cut in 1/2-inch strips. Continue process until all leaves are cut. Wash leaves thoroughly.

Pour olive oil into a large, heavy gauge pot. Add vegetables and garlic and sauté 4 minutes. Add chicken stock, meats, collard and turnip greens, vinegar, pepper flakes, and sugar. Cover pot and stir ingredients every half-hour. Periodically check pot to make certain that stock does not evaporate. Add additional stock or water if needed. Cook greens for 2 1/2 hours or until greens and meats are tender. Makes 12 servings.

Grits

Grits are by no means served just for breakfast in the South. They are an excellent side dish for any meal and are good when topped with gravies, baked in casseroles, or served in place of rice or potatoes.

6 cups chicken stock
2 cups quick grits
¼ lb. unsalted butter

Using medium heat, bring chicken stock to a rapid boil in a 2-quart pot. Add grits, whipping continuously for approximately 3 minutes. Make certain that grits do not develop lumps. Reduce to low heat. Cook grits an additional 5 minutes. Add butter and mix well. Remove pot from heat. Makes 4 servings.

Cheese Grits

4 cups chicken stock
2 cups milk
2 cups quick grits
¼ lb. butter
1 cup shredded cheddar cheese

Place a 2-quart pot on medium heat. Pour chicken stock and milk into pot and bring to a rapid boil. Add grits, whipping continuously for approximately 3 minutes. Make certain that grits do not develop lumps. Reduce heat to low heat. Cook grits for approximately 5 minutes. Add butter and cheese. Mix well. Remove pot from heat. Serve immediately. Makes 4 servings.

Baked Macaroni and Cheese

Many of my diners often describe macaroni and cheese as the ultimate comfort food. I always use a basic recipe, but depending upon the catered event or the clientele, I will sometimes add a distinctive taste to this dish by using a variety of cheeses and ingredients. I typically serve baked macaroni and cheese as a side dish, but, when served with a tossed green salad, this dish is also excellent as a entree.

1½ qt. water
1 tbsp. kosher salt
8 oz. elbow macaroni
4 oz. unsalted butter
4 tbsp. all-purpose flour
2 cups hot half-and-half
2 tsp. Dijon mustard
6 oz. mild cheddar cheese
6 oz. sharp cheddar cheese
1 tsp. onion powder
1 tsp. cayenne powder

Preheat oven to 350 degrees. Place water in a medium pot. Add salt. When water begins to boil, add pasta and stir. Return to a boil and cook uncovered 6 to 8 minutes until pasta is *al dente* or firm. Avoid overcooking. Drain pasta and set aside.

Over low heat, melt butter in a medium saucepan. The butter should be hot, but not sizzling. Add flour, stirring constantly for two minutes. Remove saucepan from heat and gradually whisk in hot half-and-half.

Return saucepan to low heat and whisk until sauce thickens. Remove saucepan from heat and stir in mustard, sharp cheddar cheese, and half of the mild cheddar cheese. Continue stirring sauce and add the onion powder and cayenne powder. Set aside.

Place pasta into a casserole dish. Pour cheese mixture over the pasta. Mix well. Place casserole dish in oven on middle rack and bake 15 minutes. Take casserole out of oven and top with remaining mild cheddar cheese. Bake an additional 6 minutes. Serve hot. Makes 8 servings.

Creamy Macaroni and Cheese

2 qt. salted water
8 oz. elbow macaroni
2 oz. unsalted butter
½ cup minced Vidalia onion
2 tbsp. plain flour
1 cup hot half-and-half
1 cup heavy cream[i1]
2 tsp. Dijon mustard
8 oz. mild cheddar cheese
8 oz. sharp cheddar cheese
1 tsp. cayenne pepper
½ tsp. salt
White pepper to taste

   Cook pasta in 2 quarts salted water at a rapid boil. Cook pasta *al dente.* Drain and set aside.
   Melt 2 ounces of butter in a large pot over low heat. Add onions and cook approximately 4 minutes or until onions are soft. Stir in flour and cook 2 minutes. Do not brown. Remove pot from heat and add hot half-and-half. Return to heat and whisk until sauce thickens. Add mustard and 8 ounces of sharp cheese and 4 ounces of mild cheese. Mix well and add cayenne, salt, and pepper.
   Mix cooked pasta into cheese sauce and place macaroni in medium casserole dish and top with remaining cheese. Bake in oven at 350 degrees for 20 minutes or until brown and bubbling. Makes 8 servings.

Three Cheese Baked Macaroni and Cheese

3 qt. water
8 oz. elbow macaroni
5 cups shredded sharp cheddar cheese
2 cups white cheddar cheese
1 tbsp. Dijon mustard
1 cup Ricotta cheese
½ cup grated Parmesan cheese
6 large eggs, beaten
3 cups milk
Salt to taste
White pepper to taste
2 tbsp. unsalted butter

Preheat oven to 350 degrees. Bring water to a rapid boil in a large pot. Add macaroni to hot water, stirring occasionally. Cook until desired tenderness, approximately 8 to 12 minutes. Drain pasta and set aside.

In a large mixing bowl, combine 3 cups of sharp cheddar, 2 cups of white cheddar, mustard, Ricotta cheese, Parmesan cheese, eggs, milk, salt and pepper, and drained macaroni. Set aside.

Grease a large casserole dish with the butter. Pour macaroni mixture into the casserole dish and cover. Bake on the middle rack of the oven for 20 minutes. Remove the macaroni from the oven and remove cover. Top with remaining sharp cheddar cheese and bake for additional 12 minutes. Serve hot. Makes 10 servings.

Dirty Rice

Dirty rice is primarily a Cajun dish. However, this rice is a featured item prepared by cooks throughout the South and by those of us with Southern roots who have relocated to other regions throughout America. This dish is popular for many reasons. It is filling, conveniently cooked in one pot, inexpensive to prepare, and most importantly, delicious. Even if chicken livers are not one of your favorite foods, you will love dirty rice. The giblets are undetectable because they become incorporated into the overall taste.

> **4 oz. unsalted butter**
> **1 cup of chicken livers, pureed in a blender**
> **4 oz. finely chopped onion**
> **1 tsp. minced fresh garlic**
> **1 cup uncooked long grain rice**
> **2½ cups heated chicken broth**
> **1 tsp. cayenne pepper**

Melt butter in a medium pot over medium heat. Add chicken livers and cook for 4 minutes. Add the onions, garlic, and rice, stirring well. Cook an additional 4 minutes. Add chicken stock and mix well. Turn heat to high and bring mixture to a boil for 5 minutes. Turn heat to low. Cook for 10 to 12 minutes until rice is fluffy and liquid is dissolved. Season with cayenne pepper. Serve hot. Makes 10 servings.

White Rice

As a child, I ate rice with dinner every night. My parents could have written a book instructing cooks on the techniques of serving rice 100 ways. They prepared rice as a side dish topped with some type of sauce, as an entree topped with some type of meat or seafood dish, or as filler in soup. If we had any rice left from dinner, we knew that our breakfast the following day would consist of eggs scrambled with rice.

Rice is a food staple in many cultures throughout the world. This grain has fed more people over a longer period of time than has any other crop. The introduction of rice to North America began somewhere around 1680, when farmers began producing a new rice seed from Madagascar on the coastal lowlands of South Carolina. This crop quickly became a lucrative source of income for planters who often referred to rice as "Carolina Gold."

There seems to be very little agreement about the best ways to cook rice since different cultures have different cooking styles and preferences. However, most cooks agree that the keys to properly cooked rice are correct proportions of rice to water and correct cooking times.

I believe that there is nothing magical about cooking rice, nor should anyone feel that cooking this grain is insurmountable. I do not buy low-grade rice, and I do not recommend washing rice because it rinses off some of the enriched vitamin coating. I prefer cooking long-grain rice with long, slender grains that stay separate and fluffy when properly cooked.

4½ cups water
1 tsp. kosher salt
1 tbsp. unsalted butter
1½ cups long grain rice

Place water in a small, heavy gauge pot. Add salt, butter, and rice. Boil rice for 5 minutes, then turn heat down to a simmer. Cover and cook 12 minutes until rice is fluffy. Makes 10 servings.

Fried Dill Pickles

4 whole dill pickles cut in ¼-inch disks
Onion salt to taste
Garlic salt to taste
Black pepper to taste
1 large egg
1 cup buttermilk
1 tsp. Worcestershire sauce
½ cup flour
½ cup yellow cornmeal
1 cup vegetable oil

Cut dill pickles into ¼-inch disks. Add onion salt, garlic salt, and black pepper. Whisk egg and buttermilk together in a medium bowl. Add Worcestershire sauce and set aside. Mix flour and cornmeal together in medium bowl and set aside.

Dip pickles in buttermilk and egg mixture. Then dip pickles into flour and corn meal mixture. Repeat process for each pickle. Place breaded pickles on medium platter until ready to fry.

Heat vegetable oil in medium frying pan to 325 degrees. Place breaded pickles into hot oil for approximately 2 to 3 minutes or until golden brown. Makes 6 servings.

Fried Green Tomatoes

4 medium green tomatoes
2 tsp. garlic powder
2 tsp. salt
1 tsp. black pepper
2 cups all-purpose flour
2 cups yellow cornmeal
2 cups buttermilk
2 large eggs
2¼ cups vegetable oil, for deep frying

Cut each tomato into 4 slices. Place in a medium pan and set aside. Combine garlic powder, salt, and black pepper. Season both sides of each tomato slice to taste. Return tomato to medium pan. Place flour in a medium bowl and set aside. Place cornmeal in a medium bowl and set aside.

Whisk buttermilk and eggs together in a medium bowl. Set aside. Heat oil in a deep, heavy gauge frying pan to 325 degrees. While oil is heating, dredge tomatoes in small batches in flour, buttermilk mixture, and cornmeal and place in medium pan. Fry tomatoes in small batches for 3 to 5 minutes or until golden brown. Serve hot. My recipe for spicy mayonnaise is an excellent dip for these fried tomatoes. Makes 4 servings.

Fresh Green Beans with Smoked Neck Bones

2 qt. chicken broth
2 lb. smoked neck bones
1 bay leaf
1 sage leaf
1 lb green beans
2 lb. unsalted butter
Cracked black pepper to taste
Salt to taste

Place chicken broth and neck bones in large pot with bay leaf and sage leaf. Cook on medium heat for approximately 1½ hours or until neck bones are tender.

Add fresh green beans, butter, salt, and pepper to taste. Cover and cook for an additional 10 minutes. Serve hot. Makes 8 servings.

Braised Kale

4 tbsp. olive oil
2 bunches of chopped small green kale
4 tbsp. minced shallots
1 tbsp. chopped fresh garlic
1 cup heated chicken stock
Salt and pepper to taste

Place olive oil, kale, shallots, and garlic in a medium pot over medium heat. Sauté for approximately 4 minutes. Add chicken stock, salt, and pepper and simmer approximately 5 minutes or until liquid evaporates. Makes 4 servings.

Kale Pasta Primavera

This is a quick yet extremely impressive side dish or main entree. This dish is a sure-fire way to get family members to eat their vegetables.

2 cups chopped kale
½ small carrot, peeled and julienne
½ green pepper, julienne
½ red pepper, julienne
½ onion, julienne
5 mushrooms, sliced
½ tsp. chopped garlic
1 cup chicken stock
1 lb. penne pasta, cooked according to instructions on package
1 tbsp. grated Parmesan cheese
2 tbsp. crumbled Gorgonzola blue cheese

Place vegetables in large sauté pan. Sauté 4 minutes. Add garlic. Continue to sauté for approximately 1 minute. Add chicken stock. Simmer 1 minute. Add cooked pasta and Parmesan cheese. Cook approximately 3 minutes. Remove from heat and add Gorgonzola blue cheese. Makes 4 servings.

Roasted Potato Duet

8 redskin potatoes, cut in half
8 purple potatoes, cut in half
Salt to taste
Cracked black pepper to taste
6 oz. olive oil
3 tbsp. chopped fresh rosemary
3 tbsp. minced fresh garlic

Place potatoes in a large bowl and season with salt and pepper. Coat potatoes with olive oil, rosemary, and garlic. Place potatoes skin-side up on a baking sheet. Cook approximately 35 minutes or until easily pierced by a fork. Serve hot. Makes 4 servings.

Stuffed Yellow Squash

With a little ingenuity, squash makes an attractive and healthy side dish for any entree. When served with stewed tomatoes, this side dish can also stand alone as an entree for the vegetarians on your guest list.

3 medium yellow squash
4 oz. unsalted butter
½ cup chopped leek bulb
½ cup chopped onions
1 tsp. finely chopped garlic
1 cup plain breadcrumbs
¾ cup grated Parmesan cheese
1 tbsp. chopped parsley
Salt and pepper to taste
¼ cup water

Cut two squash lengthwise. Using a teaspoon, remove flesh from each half of squash. Hollowed shell should be approximately ⅛ inch thick. Chop flesh into small pieces. Take the third whole squash and chop into small pieces as well. Combine chopped whole squash and flesh. Set aside.

Add butter to saucepan on medium heat. Add leeks. Cook for approximately two minutes, stirring occasionally. Add onions and cook approximately three minutes or until tender. Add chopped garlic and chopped squash. Cook until tender, approximately four minutes. Add bread crumbs, Parmesan cheese, and parsley. Stir mixture. Remove from heat and season with salt and pepper to taste. Allow mixture to cool for approximately two minutes.

Stuff each hollowed squash with vegetable mixture. Place each squash stuffed-side up in a casserole dish with ¼ cup of water. Cover and bake in 350-degree oven approximately 20 minutes or until squash is tender. Remove from oven. I suggest serving squash with stewed tomatoes. Makes 2 servings.

Stewed Tomatoes

Stewed tomatoes add another dimension to any meal. Whenever I want to add a little lift to any dish, I simply top it off with stewed tomatoes. They are fabulous when served with stuffed yellow squash or served over grits or rice.

3 medium vine-ripened tomatoes
1 qt. water
¼ cup vegetable oil
½ cup chopped white onions
1 tsp. finely chopped fresh garlic
½ cup chopped celery
½ cup chopped green peppers
3 tsp. sugar
1 tbsp. chopped fresh parsley
1 tsp. chopped fresh thyme
1 bay leaf
Salt and pepper to taste

Score bottom of each tomato with x-shaped marks. Place tomatoes in boiling water and cook approximately two minutes. Remove tomatoes from boiling water and shock with cold water. Using scored x marks as a guideline, peel skin from tomatoes, starting from bottom. After removing skin, chop tomatoes and set aside.

Add vegetable oil to saucepan over medium heat. Add chopped onions and cook for approximately three minutes, stirring occasionally. Add chopped tomatoes, garlic, celery, green peppers, and sugar. Stir mixture. Simmer for ten minutes. Add parsley, thyme, and bay leaf. Stir mixture. Simmer for approximately 10 to 15 minutes. Season with salt and pepper to taste. Makes 2 servings.

Yellow Squash Casserole

3 oz. unsalted butter
5 lb. sliced yellow squash
1 qt. half-and-half
3 cups crushed saltine crackers
4 cups grated sharp cheese
8 large eggs, lightly beaten
Salt and pepper to taste
¼ tsp. grated fresh nutmeg

Preheat oven to 325 degrees. Melt butter in a heavy gauge saucepan. Add squash and sauté for 3 minutes on medium heat. Spread squash in a 9 x 13 baking dish. Sprinkle crackers over squash. Set aside.

Combine milk, cheese, and eggs in a mixing bowl. Mix well. Add salt, pepper, and nutmeg. Mix thoroughly. Pour liquid mixture over crackers and squash. Cover with aluminum foil. Bake for 35 to 40 minutes until center is set. Remove from oven. Serve hot. Makes 12 servings.

Candied Sweet Potatoes

3 lb. sweet potatoes
½ cup brown sugar
¼ cup granulated sugar
1 cup fresh pineapple juice
1 cup cold water
1 tbsp. ground cinnamon
1 cup fresh-squeezed orange juice

Preheat oven to 400 degrees. Peel sweet potatoes and cut into 1-inch disks. Place sweet potatoes in cold water until all potatoes are peeled and cut.

Place sweet potatoes in deep baking dish. Add sugar, pineapple juice, orange juice, and water. Sprinkle ground cinnamon over top of potatoes. Cover and bake in oven for approximately 40 to 50 minutes or until sweet potatoes are fork tender. Makes 6 servings.

Sweet Potato and Apple Casserole

4 Granny Smith apples, cored, peeled, quartered, and sliced
3 medium yams, peeled and sliced in ¼-inch rounds
1 tbsp. cinnamon
¼ tsp. nutmeg
8 oz. dark brown sugar
8 oz. apple juice
4 oz. unsalted butter, cut into small pieces

In a casserole dish combine the apples and yams. Sprinkle the cinnamon, nutmeg, and brown sugar over the apples and yams. Pour apple juice over the yam mixture. Add butter to mixture. Cover and bake at 325 degrees 30 to 35 minutes until yams are tender. Makes 6 servings.

Sauces, Salsas, Relishes, and Dressings

I frequently serve a sauce with many of my appetizers and entrees. A good sauce can transform an ordinary dish to an extraordinary dining experience. I often recall occasions when one of the most memorable parts of a finely-catered event was the sauce that I used to enhance the flavor of an appetizer or an entree. Throughout the world, it is not uncommon to see diners using a piece of bread or the final morsel on their plate to capture the last drops of sauce on their plates. This is equally true amongst many American Southerners. Some Southerners refer to this behavior of capturing their sauce as either mopping or "sopping" up their sauce. I strongly believe that good sauces are the pinnacle of all cooking.

I remember spending many hours learning the art of perfecting the consistency of different sauces. Each time I was learning to make a new sauce, my chef instructor required me to place a sample of that sauce in the center of a paper plate. He would then tilt the plate from side to side, allowing the sauce to run in each pointed direction. The process of perfecting my sauces entailed walking back and forth seeking my instructor's approval. I can still recall how extremely frustrated I became during these initial experiences, not to mention almost wearing out the soles of my shoes. However, once I mastered the art of creating sauces, I quickly excelled to the top of my class.

I do not want the novice cook to become intimidated by the vast number of sauces. Although the combinations of ingredients seem endless, all sauces stem from the same basic methods. A sauce works like a seasoning. A good sauce should complement and enhance the flavor and texture of the food it accompanies. An exceptional sauce must never overpower the food.

A few key tips in creating a good sauce include using the proper utensils, high quality ingredients, a good stock, and patience. The saucepan should be of heavy metal that holds and distributes the heat evenly. Sauces scorch easily in lightweight pans, even with constant stirring.

Occasionally, I also use salsas to perk up dishes. Salsas are quick and easy to make, and customers immensely enjoy the unexpected treat that these sauces provide. When I initially introduced salsas to my menus, several guests thought I would limit the selections to a cold, spicy sauce containing tomatoes. However, I began serving non-tomato-based salsas using fresh fruits or a medley of vegetables, to my customers' delight. They adore the variety of homespun salsas that I use to liven up meats, poultry, fish, and appetizers.

Salsas not only perk up a dish but also can liven up any festive occasion. I recollect catering a Halloween party for celebrities and individuals who work in the entertainment industry. The buffet consisted of hors d'oeuvres, fresh fruits, and cheese platters. I also included a small salsa station with taco chips. Within a few minutes, a small crowd began to gather around the salsa station. Some of the guests behaved like excited children, encouraging each other to taste one salsa after another. The host became curious about the rousing pitch that emanated from the buffet table and approached the area to see what was happening. For approximately twenty minutes, the focus of the party revolved around the salsa station.

I hope the following recipes will inspire the creative cook to think outside the box.

Brown Sauce

4 tbsp. unsalted butter
¼ cup chopped carrots
¼ cup chopped celery
1 medium onion, chopped
4 tbsp. all-purpose flour
1 qt. warm brown stock
2 sprigs parsley
1 sprig thyme
1 bay leaf
1 clove garlic, chopped
Salt and pepper to taste

Melt butter in medium saucepan on low heat. Add carrots, celery, and onion. Continue to cook 5 minutes, stirring vegetables with a wooden spoon, until vegetables are golden brown. Add flour and cook an additional 5 minutes. Add stock and mix well. Add parsley, thyme, bay leaf, and garlic. Cook an additional 5 minutes. Strain sauce into another saucepan. Heat and season with salt and pepper. Makes 12 servings.

Sauces, Salsas, Relishes, and Dressings

Chicken Sauce

4 tbsp. unsalted butter
4 tbsp. all-purpose flour
3 cups heated chicken stock
1 medium onion, finely chopped
1 tsp. chopped fresh thyme
1 tsp. minced fresh garlic
1 tsp. ground sage
1 tbsp. Gravy Master®
Salt and black pepper to taste

Heat butter on low heat in a heavy gauge saucepot. Stir in flour continuously for approximately 3 minutes until flour is light brown. Add stock, onions, thyme, garlic, sage, and Gravy Master®.

Bring gravy to a boil for approximately 2 minutes. Reduce heat and simmer 10 to 12 minutes until onions are tender. Season with salt and pepper to taste. Serve hot. Makes 8 to 12 servings.

Honey Mustard Sauce

8 oz. honey
2 tbsp. Dijon mustard
1 tbsp. sugar
2 oz. red wine vinegar
2 tbsp. soy sauce

Combine all ingredients and mix well. Serve at room temperature. Makes 4 to 6 servings.

Mustard Sauce

This is a magnificent topping for fish, chicken, or pork. I strongly suggest serving this sauce with baked swordfish.

12 oz. chicken stock
4 oz. Dijon mustard
1 tbsp. balsamic vinegar
1 sprig rosemary

Combine all ingredients in a saucepan. Place pan on medium heat. Stir ingredients for 30 seconds. Simmer sauce for 5 minutes and serve hot over fish or chicken. Makes 4 servings.

Remoulade Sauce

1 cup mayonnaise
1 tbsp. sweet relish
1 tsp. fresh minced garlic
2 tbsp. tomato ketchup
1 tsp. small capers
1 tbsp. minced anchovies

In a small bowl, mix all ingredients together. Stir well. Refrigerate until ready to use. Makes 5 servings.

Pesto Sauce

Pesto sauce varies from cook to cook. Some cooks add an extra punch to their sauce by increasing the amount of garlic. Other cooks use walnuts in place of pine nuts. The one ingredient that is constant in any pesto sauce is the predominance of basil.

During the course of the 11 years that I have cooked at my restaurant, I have introduced many different types of sauces and new seasonings to my customers. Initially, many of my customers were reluctant to try some of the daily specials if they were unfamiliar with the seasonings or herbs. I would offer samples of some of the sauces and spend time in the dining room educating some of my customers while coaxing others to try new dishes. Eventually, customers began asking about the specials before the host could seat them.

Many of my customers have developed an appreciation for my style of cooking and are now willing to break out of their traditional eating pattern and try new dishes.

The great thing about most of my recipes is that the taste surpasses the amount of time that it takes to prepare the entrees.

½ cup fresh basil, washed well
2 tbsp. grated Parmesan cheese
2 tbsp. toasted pine nuts
¼ cup olive oil
1 tsp. minced fresh garlic
Salt and pepper to taste

Combine all ingredients in food processor. Pulse 3 minutes until ingredients form a thick sauce. Pour sauce into a small bowl. Use immediately or cover and refrigerate. Makes 4 servings.

Strawberry Sauce

1 cup water
1½ cups frozen strawberries
½ cup sugar
2 tbsp. amaretto liqueur

In a medium pot over low heat, combine water, strawberries, sugar, and liqueur. Cook for 15 minutes. Remove from heat and allow strawberries to cool. After strawberries have cooled, place in a blender and puree for 4 minutes. Serve cold. Makes 6 servings.

Tartar Sauce

This tartar sauce recipe is amazing with most seafood entrees and appetizers.

1 cup mayonnaise
¼ cup grated onions
1 tbsp. pickle relish
1 tbsp. Worcestershire sauce
1 tsp. lemon juice
1 anchovy, diced

Combine all ingredients in a small mixing bowl. Mix well. Makes 4 servings.

Yogurt Sauce

Throughout my life, I have heard that one of the secrets of long life is eating yogurt frequently. I do not know if this is true, but I do know it makes a good sauce. Even if you are reticent about the taste of yogurt, add this sauce to your fish and I am certain that you will join the ranks of perennial yogurt eaters.

    4 oz. chopped fresh dill
    4 oz. chopped fresh parsley
    4 oz. chopped fresh cilantro
    1 tsp. grated lime zest
    Juice from 1 lime
    1 tsp. grated fresh ginger
    1 tsp. finely chopped Jalapeno pepper
    8 oz. plain yogurt

Combine all ingredients and mix well. Refrigerate until ready to use. Makes 4 servings.

Pear and Apple Salsa

Adding this salsa to a basic meal can change a simple entree into a sophisticated dish. I use this salsa with grilled pork chops in place of applesauce.

    1 Bosc pear, chopped and core removed
    1 red delicious apple, chopped and core removed
    ½ red onion, finely chopped
    ¼ tsp. chili flakes
    4 oz. chopped cilantro
    Juice from 1 lime, seeds removed
    Salt to taste
    White pepper to taste

In a small glass bowl, combine pear, apple, onion, chili, cilantro, and lime juice. Toss ingredients. Season with salt and white pepper to taste. Makes 4 servings.

Watermelon Salsa

Most Southerners enjoy biting into a juicy slice of watermelon. This fruit is a true symbol of summer. I enjoy eating watermelons so much that I came up with this wonderful recipe one day. This summer salsa is an excellent way to use this fruit when grilling fish or meats.

2 cups diced seedless watermelon
1 tsp. minced Jalapeno pepper
2 tsp. finely diced red onion
1 tbsp. finely diced green pepper
¼ tsp. minced fresh garlic
Juice from 1 lime
¼ tsp. chopped fresh mint
Salt to taste
Cracked black pepper to taste

Mix all ingredients in a medium bowl. Cover and marinate in refrigerator 30 minutes before serving. Serve at room temperature. Makes 4 servings.

Cucumber Relish

2 large tomatoes, finely chopped
2 medium cucumbers, peeled, seeded, and chopped
2 tbsp. finely chopped cilantro
2 tbsp. finely chopped onion
1 pickled Jalapeno pepper, seeded and finely chopped
2 tbsp. lemon juice
Salt and black pepper to taste

Combine all ingredients in a mixing bowl. Cover and refrigerate until needed. Makes 6 servings.

Black-Eyed-Pea Relish

6 cups of water
½ cup dry black-eyed peas
8 cups cold water
¼ cup finely chopped ripe tomatoes
¼ cup finely chopped Spanish onions
¼ cup finely chopped red onions
¼ cup finely chopped green pepper
1 tsp. minced Jalapeno pepper
1 tbsp. hot sauce
2 tbsp. fresh lime juice
½ cup chili sauce
1 tbsp. chopped cilantro
Salt and pepper to taste

Place peas in a medium mixing bowl. Pour 6 cups of water into bowl with peas and soak peas for 1 hour. Sort out any unwanted material and rinse peas well. Drain water from peas.

Place peas in a medium pot. Pour in 8 cups of cold water. Simmer peas on medium heat approximately 30 minutes or until peas are tender. Do not overcook. Drain peas and set aside. Allow peas to cool.

In a medium mixing bowl, combine the remaining ingredients. Mix well and refrigerate 30 minutes. Serve chilled. Makes 8 servings.

Breads and Biscuits

BREADS AND BISCUITS

I cannot imagine eating a meal without a piece of bread or a biscuit. Southerners use breads as a precursor to most meals or for catching that last bit of sauce or gravy on a plate. I know that there is a movement at large encouraging individuals to refrain from eating carbohydrates, but my customers would run me out of town if I told them that I was no longer serving corn bread or biscuits. I have customers who purchase extra pieces of corn bread to either eat with their meals or take home for a snack.

Biscuits are what make Sunday morning breakfast so special. When I am feeling imaginative, I add fruits, cheeses, or other ingredients to my bread and biscuit recipes. When I think about the boundless recipes that I have created by simply changing a few ingredients, I do not understand why more home cooks do not bake bread.

I know that it is convenient to purchase prepared biscuits and breads; however, there is a minimal amount of work required to make these products "from scratch." Taking a few extra minutes, anyone can create superior products.

Though time is a commodity for many individuals, the aromatic smells created from baking the recipes in this section will certainly help to slow down even the most active individual. When eaten in moderation, most breads should not add inches to the coveted waistline.

Banana Nut Bread

2 cups all-purpose flour
1 tbsp. baking powder
8 oz. unsalted butter, softened
1 tbsp. vegetable oil
1 cup sugar
3 ripe bananas
2 large eggs
¼ cup milk
½ cup pecans

Preheat oven to 325 degrees. In a small bowl, sift the flour and baking powder together and set aside. Whip butter, oil, sugar, and bananas in a separate mixing bowl using an electric mixer on medium speed. Add eggs one at a time. Stop mixer and scrape batter from sides of bowl. Add flour mixture and milk. Turn mixer to medium speed and whip for approximately 5 minutes. Stop mixer and stir in pecans.

Pour batter into 9 x 5 x 3 greased loaf pan. Bake 55 minutes or until toothpick comes out clean when inserted into the center of bread. Serve warm. Makes 12 servings.

Buttermilk Biscuits

Every Sunday morning, my customers enjoy these biscuits with butter and jelly or syrup and served with fish and grits or salmon croquettes. I also serve these biscuits as an open-faced appetizer topped with barbecue shrimp. When I use them as an appetizer, I cut the biscuits into smaller disks. Some customers enjoy these biscuits with their dinner in place of corn bread.

2 cups self-rising flour
1 tsp. baking powder
¼ tsp. salt
2 tbsp. sugar
4 oz. shortening, chilled
2 tbsp. unsalted butter, chilled ⅔ cup buttermilk
1 egg, beaten

Preheat oven to 375 degrees. In a medium bowl, sift together dry ingredients except sugar and three tablespoons of flour for dusting. Cut sugar and butter into sifted flour. Mix until flour resembles tiny peas. Add shortening. Add buttermilk and stir lightly.

Remove dough from bowl. Place dough on floured board and knead gently for approximately 1 minute. Pat and roll dough to desired thickness. Cut dough with cookie cutter. Place the biscuits on ungreased baking sheet.

Brush biscuits with beaten egg and bake on middle rack 12 to15 minutes or until biscuits are golden brown. Cut biscuits in half, separating the top from the bottom. Makes 8 biscuits.

Waffles

Although diners typically associate waffles with breakfast foods, I serve these fluffy disks with fried chicken, pork chops, and even fried fish. This is an award-winning recipe when coupled with fried chicken. Feel free to serve waffles for breakfast, brunch, and dinner. New Southern cuisine is creative cuisine.

> 10 oz. flour
> ½ tsp. salt
> 1 tbsp. baking powder
> 1 tsp. vanilla extract
> 4 egg yolks, beaten
> 8 oz. milk
> 4 oz. unsalted melted butter
> 4 egg whites
> 2 oz. sugar

In a medium mixing bowl sift together flour, salt, and baking powder. Add vanilla extract, egg yolks, milk, and butter. Mix well. Set batter aside.

In a small mixing bowl, beat the egg whites for 3 minutes or until they form soft peaks. Use an electric mixer if available. Add sugar and beat until stiff peaks form. Fold egg white mixture into batter.

Pour batter into preheated waffle iron. Batter should reach the surface of the waffle iron. Close waffle iron and cook batter. Remove waffle when timer or bell rings after approximately 3 minutes. Makes 4 to 6 servings.

Crusty Skillet Corn Bread

2 cups yellow corn meal
½ cup all-purpose flour
½ tsp. salt
½ tsp. baking soda
3 tbsp. sugar
2 tsp. baking powder
4 eggs
1¼ cups buttermilk
½ stick butter

Mix all of the dry ingredients together in a medium bowl. Set aside. In a small bowl, stir eggs into buttermilk. Add egg and buttermilk mixture to dry mixture.

Melt butter inside heavy iron skillet and coat skillet on all sides with the butter. Pour remaining butter from skillet into corn bread batter and mix thoroughly. Pour corn bread batter into hot skillet and bake in a 350-degree oven. Cook bread 25 to 30 minutes or until it has a golden brown crust. Makes 8 servings.

Sweet Potato Bread

This sweet potato bread comes together in a jiffy. It goes beautifully with fried chicken or pork chops. I also serve it as a breakfast bread. It is great with a cup of tea or coffee or even a glass of milk.

    3½ cups all-purpose flour
    2 tsp. baking soda
    1 tsp. baking powder
    1 tsp. salt
    1 tsp. cinnamon
    1 tsp. nutmeg
    1 tsp. allspice
    ½ tsp. ground cloves
    2½ cups sugar
    1 cup brown sugar
    1 cup vegetable oil
    3 large eggs
    2 sweet potatoes
    1 cup chopped pecans
    1 cup golden raisins

Bake 2 sweet potatoes until tender, approximately 35 to 40 munutes. This should yield 2 cups of baked sweet potatoe.

In a medium bowl, sift together the first eight ingredients and set aside. In a second medium bowl, combine the sugars, oil, eggs, and cooked sweet potatoes. Mix until smooth, approximately 4 minutes. Add chopped pecans and golden raisins. Mix an additional 2 minutes. Add the sifted ingredients to the sweet potato mixture and mix for approximately 4 more minutes.

Pour mixture into a non-stick loaf pan. Bake for 50 to 60 minutes or until an inserted toothpick comes out clean. Cool bread at least 30 minutes before removing from pan. Slice and serve. Makes 10 to 12 servings.

Sweet Potato Pancakes with Pecans

What could be more Southern than sweet potatoes and pecans? My family had a pecan tree in our backyard. We ate plenty of pecan pies and cakes topped with pecans, and pecans roasted in the fireplace always served as a quick evening snack. I recall a few occasions when I became ill from eating pecans before they ripened.

I must honestly say that some of my friends and I mischievously used pecans as arsenal when we played games of combat. Somehow we felt that we were not disobeying our parents who frequently advised us not to throw rocks.

These pancakes are outrageously delicious when topped with strawberries and whipped cream. Many of my customers also eat these pancakes with fried chicken, rather than with traditional breakfast meats.

2 sweet potatoes
¼ cup sugar
1½ cups milk
½ cup heavy cream
4 large eggs
2½ cups all-purpose flour
¼ tsp. baking soda
4 tsp. baking powder
½ tsp. kosher salt
1½ tsp. ground cinnamon
¼ tsp. fresh grated nutmeg
16 oz. unsalted melted butter
½ cup chopped pecans
1 pint fresh strawberries, optional topping
Whipped cream, optional topping

Bake sweet potatoes until tender, approximately 25-30 minutes. Allow potatoes to cool, then remove peeling from sweet potatoes.

In a large mixing bowl, cream together sweet potatoes, sugar, milk, and heavy cream for approximately 4 minutes. Break the 4 eggs, separating the yolks from the whites. Set the egg whites aside. Thoroughly mix in 1 egg yolk at a time. In a separate bowl, sift together all dry ingredients. Mix the dry ingredients into the sweet potato mixture until all ingredients are blended thoroughly. Add 12 ounces of melted butter and pecans. Mix thoroughly.

Place egg whites in a separate bowl and beat until whites form a stiff peak. Using a rubber spatula, gently fold egg whites into sweet potato mixture.

Heat pancake grill or non-stick frying pan on medium heat. Add the remaining butter as needed to lightly grease pan. Scoop potato mixture using a 6-ounce ladle or a #24 scoop and place batter onto a lightly greased griddle or pan. Turn pancakes when edges look brown and bubbles appear on top. Turn each pancake one time, browning on both sides. Add strawberry and whipped cream topping if desired. Makes 5 to 6 servings.

Desserts

DESSERTS

Southerners love their desserts. To be quite honest, I have never met anyone who does not enjoy ending a scrumptious meal followed by a delectable dessert. I have several customers who frequently request containers to take home half of their uneaten meals, explaining that they are saving room for dessert.

Other customers who eat their entire meal often order several desserts to take home to eat at a later time. Needless to say, I spend a considerable amount of time baking desserts. I often amaze new customers when they find out that I both cook and bake (most chef's specialize in one or the other). I bake all of my desserts. Baking helps to relax my mind and is a welcomed change from the accelerated pace of cooking on the line (behind the stoves) in the restaurant.

I often feel like a chemist when I am in the kitchen creating new dishes, adding a little bit of this and a touch of that. Cooking is a science. This statement is particularly true when it comes to baking. I cannot stress the importance of accuracy when baking. The slightest difference in proportions or procedures can mean significant differences in the final product. I *always* use measuring cups and spoons whenever I bake. I recommend that anyone who attempts to bake does the same.

In this section, I present an array of recipes for desserts that my customers highly favor. These recipes are appropriate for every occasion and taste. Baking leaves very little margin for error, so I have taken special measures to adapt these recipes to ensure the likelihood of success. These unpretentious cobblers, pies, and cakes definitely capture the flavors of the South. I am confident that everyone will enjoy these irresistible desserts.

Banana Pudding

My mother often made banana pudding when I was a child. Though she took short cuts and prepared this dessert using instant pudding, I thought her banana pudding was absolutely delicious. I did not know what I was missing. I did not know that she could have created custard from scratch that would have had a substantially better taste.

I am always trying to create irresistible treats, and I cannot fathom cooking a dessert using boxed pudding. Creating my own custard enables me to control the flavors and the amount of sugar used.

Preparing custard only requires a few minutes and the taste is phenomenal. Banana pudding is one dessert that I sell out daily. I have some customers who purchase several orders at a time and often joke that all of the orders are for themselves, rather than for sharing with family members. This banana pudding is so delicious that a few customers purchase this dessert even when the custard has not had a chance to set. They tell me they do not care about the texture; they simply love the taste!

1 qt. heavy cream
¼ cup cold water
2 tbsp. cornstarch
1 cup sugar
2 tbsp. vanilla extract
¼ cup amaretto liqueur
¼ cup banana liqueur
4 egg yolks
1 box vanilla wafers, approximately 12 oz.
6 ripe bananas, sliced

Using a heavy-gauge medium saucepan, bring heavy cream to a boil. Reduce heat.

In a small bowl, mix water and cornstarch. Whisk mixture into the hot cream. Add sugar, vanilla, and liqueurs, whisking continuously. Add egg yolks, continuously whisking the custard. Let the custard simmer for approximately 5 minutes, continuing to whisk. Remove from heat.

In a medium casserole pan or glass bowl, layer the wafers and the bananas. Alternate a layer of wafers with a layer of bananas. Wafers should be used for the first and last layers. Pour custard over wafers and sliced bananas. Refrigerate, allowing the banana pudding to set. Makes 5 servings.

Almost Sam's Pound Cake

The old-fashioned pound cake may have gained its popularity and its name because it presented few challenges to make and required one pound of its primary ingredients. The original recipe called for one pound of butter, one pound of sugar, one pound of eggs, and one pound of cake flour. Practically anyone could make this cake.

Pound cakes can take on a whole new life by simply adding different flavorings: nuts, dried fruits, cream cheese, sour cream, fresh fruit toppings, or chocolate. It is also possible to reduce some of the calories using vegetable oil and sugar substitutes. When my father, Sam Jones, prepared this cake, neither he nor his guests expressed any concern about their weight.

For some odd reason, whenever my father baked this cake, he would slam the oven door, causing the cake to collapse inward! His method was a direct contradiction to everything that I learned in school. My baking instructor warned us not to open ovens or disturb cakes until they were finished rising and were partially browned. A cake's structure is very fragile, and proper baking conditions are essential if the baker desires a superb product. Disturbing cakes before they set will cause them to fall. That is why this recipe is almost that of my father's, because I definitely do not suggest stomping or slamming oven doors.

Interestingly, the imploded pound cakes were one of my father's signature items that family members still talk about and desire.

3½ cups cake flour
1½ tsp. baking powder
1 lb. unsalted butter, room temperature
4 oz. cream cheese, room temperature
2 oz. vegetable oil
5 large eggs
2 tbsp. lemon extract
Baking release spray

Preheat oven to 350 degrees. In a small bowl, combine flour and baking powder. Set aside. In an electric mixing bowl on medium speed, cream together the butter, cream cheese, and vegetable oil for 8 minutes.

Add the eggs one at a time, beating well after each addition. Stop mixer and scrape the sides of the bowl to avoid lumps in the mixture. Turn the mixer to medium-high speed and mix for an additional two minutes. Remove bowl and stir in lemon extract.

Spray a bundt pan with baking release spray. Pour batter into pan and bake 50 to 60 minutes or until a toothpick comes out clean when inserted into center of the cake. Makes 8 servings.

Sautéed Bananas

I use this recipe on vanilla ice cream, waffles, or pancakes. The alcohol in the amaretto and banana liqueurs burns away while sautéing the bananas, leaving an intriguing blend of the liqueurs and the intrinsic flavor of the fruit. For special occasions, I place two scoops of ice cream in a brandy glass and spoon the hot banana mixture on top of the ice cream.

Serving this simply prepared dessert in fancy glasses always helps to make guests feel extra special.

2 tbsp. butter
2 medium ripe bananas, sliced
¼ cup banana liqueur
¼ cup amaretto liqueur
2 tbsp. sugar
1 tbsp. ground cinnamon

Melt butter in medium sauté pan. Add sliced bananas. Add banana and amaretto liqueurs, then add sugar and cinnamon. Cook for approximately 3 minutes. Remove from heat. Pour over ice cream, waffles, or pancakes. Makes 2 servings.

Cheesecake

8 oz. graham cracker crumbs
¼ cup finely grounded pecans
12 oz. + 2 tbsp. sugar
4 tbsp. melted unsalted butter
2½ lb. softened cream cheese
3 tbsp. cornstarch
½ tsp. almond extract
½ tsp. vanilla extract
½ cup sour cream
4 large eggs

Preheat oven to 350 degrees. Combine crumbs, pecans, sugar, and butter. Mix well and set aside.

Use an electric mixer on medium speed to blend the cream cheese, corn starch, almond and vanilla extracts, and sour cream for approximately five minutes or until well blended. Add eggs one at a time and blend well after each addition.

Press crumb mixture into the bottom and sides of a 9-inch spring-form pan. Pour cream cheese mixture over crust and bake for 1 hour and 10 minutes or until center is almost set. Refrigerate 4 hours or overnight. Makes 8 servings.

Chocolate Cheesecake

For some individuals, chocolate is the ultimate indulgence. A hint of chocolate can transform simple sweets into sophisticated classics.

> 2 cups chocolate cookie crumbs
> 2 tbsp. sugar
> ¼ cup melted unsalted butter
> 2 oz. bittersweet chocolate
> 8 oz. semi-sweet chocolate
> 1½ lb. cream cheese, room temperature
> 2½ tbsp. cornstarch
> 2 oz. sour cream
> 1½ tsp. vanilla extract
> 3 large eggs

Preheat oven to 325 degrees. Combine the cookie crumbs, sugar, and butter in a small bowl. Mix well until the crumbs are moist. Place crumbs into a 9-inch spring-form pan. Coat the bottom evenly with crumbs and spread crumbs about 1 inch high up the side of the pan. Set the pan aside.

Put the bittersweet and semi-sweet chocolate in the top of a double boiler and set over simmering water until the chocolate melts. Remove the chocolate from the heat and stir until smooth. Set aside.

In a mixing bowl, combine the cream cheese, cornstarch, sour cream, and vanilla extract. Mix on medium speed approximately 6 minutes. Stop mixer every 2 minutes and scrape the sides of the bowl to prevent lumps in the mixture. Add eggs one at a time, mixing well after every addition. Beat an additional three minutes until smooth.

Remove bowl from mixer and blend chocolate in well. Pour mixture into crust and back 60 to 65 minutes until the center is set or the center still jiggles slightly. Cover cake and refrigerate overnight. Cheesecake will set as it cools. Makes 8 servings.

Desserts

Peanut Butter Cheesecake with Peanut Butter Cookie Crust

10 peanut butter cookies
1 tsp. sugar
3 tbsp. melted butter
Vegetable oil spray
2 lb. cream cheese
1 cup creamy peanut butter
1½ cups granulated sugar
1 tbsp. all-purpose flour
4 large eggs
2 tsp. vanilla extract

Begin by preparing the crust. Crumble peanut butter cookies in a small bowl. Add sugar and melted butter. Mix all ingredients well. Spray a 9 x 3 spring-form pan with the vegetable oil. Place ingredients into the bottom of the pan and, using fingertips or a spoon, press ingredients to form crust.

Preheat oven to 350 degrees. Combine cream cheese and peanut butter in a large mixing bowl. Using a wire whip, beat the mixture in an electric mixer until smooth. Gradually add sugar and flour. Beat on medium speed until sugar and flour are well incorporated into the cream cheese and peanut butter mixture. Scrape batter from sides of bowl before adding eggs. Add eggs gradually and continue to beat on medium speed for 3 minutes until mixture is smooth. Add vanilla extract and continue to mix 3 additional minutes.

Pour mixture into prepared cookie crust. Place cheesecake in oven on center rack. Bake cheesecake in a water bath for approximately 2 hours at 350 degrees or until tip of a knife comes out clean when inserted in center of cake. Makes 8 servings.

Chocolate Pecan Pie

This is a delectable twist on a traditional Southern dessert. Typically, pecan pie is very sweet, the very reason why some of my customers would forgo selecting this dessert. However, when I began adding the chocolate, my sales of this dessert increased.

The chocolate tones down the sweetness, creating a wonderful dessert for chocolate lovers and for those who enjoy pecan pie. The bourbon adds an intriguing flavor. Now and then, I use wines and spirits when cooking some of my dishes and desserts to enhance natural flavor, but I do not overwhelm the taste. Moderation is the key to successfully adding these ingredients. Diners can be worry free because the alcohol evaporates during the cooking or baking process, leaving only a subtle flavor.

3 large eggs
½ cup dark brown sugar
½ cup white sugar
¾ cup dark karo syrup
1 tsp. vanilla extract
2 tbsp. unsalted butter
2 oz. bourbon
4 oz. semi-sweet chocolate
1¼ cup shelled pecans
1 9-inch, unbaked, deep-dish pie crust

In a large bowl, combine eggs, dark brown and white sugar, syrup, and vanilla extract. Set aside.

In a double boiler, melt butter, bourbon, and chocolate together. Allow to cool about 2 minutes. Fold chocolate mixture into egg mixture. Add pecans and pour mixture into pie crust.

Bake 45 to 55 minutes or until knife inserted halfway between center and edge comes out clean. Makes 8 servings.

Chocolate Cake

The climax of most special occasions always seems to center around the cake. This cake, with its rich, delicious chocolate frosting, always brings wide smiles to customers' faces, whether served during a birthday celebration or for a special anniversary.

In addition to using baking release spray, I also place circles of wax paper on the bottom of the cake pans. This makes removing the cakes from the pans much easier.

3 cups cake flour
¾ cup cocoa powder
2 tsp. baking powder
¼ tsp. baking soda
1 tsp. salt
8 oz. vegetable oil
2 cups sugar
2 large eggs
2 cups buttermilk
½ tsp. vanilla extract
½ tsp. almond extract
Baking release spray

Preheat oven to 350 degrees. In a medium bowl, sift together the flour, cocoa powder, baking powder, baking soda, and salt. Set aside.

Using an electric mixer, blend vegetable oil and sugar in a medium bowl. Whip approximately 3 minutes until smooth. Add eggs one at a time and continue mixing. Add flour mixture one cup at a time, alternating with buttermilk. Beat approximately 3 minutes. Add vanilla and almond extracts and continue to mix for an additional minute. Stop mixer and spray two 9-inch cake pans with baking release spray.

Pour batter into cake pans, evenly distributing cake batter. Bake cakes on middle rack 25 to 30 minutes or until a toothpick inserted in the center of the cake comes out clean. Allow cake to cool before applying chocolate frosting. Make the chocolate frosting while baking the cake. Makes 8 servings.

Chocolate Frosting

2 oz. butter, softened
2 oz. cream cheese, softened
6 oz. powdered sugar
4 tbsp. cocoa powder
1 tsp. vanilla extract

In an electric mixer on low speed, whisk together the butter, cream cheese, powdered sugar, and cocoa powder for 8 minutes or until smooth. Turn mixer off and scrape ingredients from sides of mixing bowl. Add vanilla extract and turn mixer on medium speed and whisk for an additional 5 minutes. Spread icing on cake. Makes 8 servings.

Peach Cobbler

Fruit desserts are popular throughout the world. Cobbler is one of the most popular Southern desserts. Cobblers are very similar to fruit pies. They are made in large baking pans, but without bottom crusts. The funny thing about many of my customers is that when they place an order, they always tell the staff to make certain that they give them a lot of crust. To satisfy their requests, I have had to increase the thickness of the crust of my cobblers when I bake for the restaurant. My wife often tells me that I should bake pies because everyone would then have enough crust without my having to change my cobbler recipe. This recipe is made without the additional crust.

Although I use several fruit fillings when baking cobblers, peach is my favorite. Georgia is one of the three states in America that produces peaches, so it is difficult not to love peaches when you are raised in Georgia. I must have eaten at least one peach daily as a child. Now that I live in New York, I look forward to the first shipment of summer peaches from my home state.

Topping

5 cups all-purpose flour
1 tbsp. yellow corn meal
5½ tsp. baking powder
1 tsp. baking soda
2 cups sugar
1 tsp. salt
8 oz. melted unsalted butter
2 cups buttermilk
2 tbsp. vanilla extract
2 tbsp. all-purpose flour, for dusting

Filling

12 peaches, each peeled, pitted, and sliced into 6 wedges
1 cup dark brown sugar
1½ cup granulated sugar
2 tbsp. ground cinnamon
1 tsp. ground fresh nutmeg
4 oz. unsalted butter, cut into small pieces
8 oz. peach nectar
4 tbsp. cornstarch

To make the topping, sift together flour, cornmeal, baking powder, baking soda, sugar, and salt in a mixing bowl. Add butter, milk, and vanilla extract and mix well.

Dust a table or a board with 2 tablespoons flour. Knead dough for 2 minutes. Roll out dough the size of the baking pan. Set aside.

To make the filling, combine sugars, cinnamon, nutmeg, and butter in a heavy gauge pot on medium heat. Cook for 4 minutes. While sugar mixture is cooking, combine peach nectar, peaches, and cornstarch in small mixing bowl. Stir well. Add peach nectar mixture to pot and cook for an additional 4 minutes. Turn off heat and pour peach mixture into 9 x 13-inch casserole dish and top with dough. Bake for 25 to 30 minutes until top is golden brown. Makes 12 servings.

Peach Pie

A peach pie is another dessert that always captivates guests. I love Georgia peaches and tend to use this fruit in salads, as toppings for pancakes and waffles, and in salsas. I enjoy other fruit pies, but there is something about a peach pie that transports me to an innocent time in my life. I often use this pie crust when making my pies.

Peach Filling

6 large peaches, sliced, peeled, and pitted
½ cup light brown sugar
¾ cups granulated sugar
1 tsp. fresh ground cinnamon
¼ tsp. fresh grated nutmeg
½ cup all-purpose flour
2 tbsp. sweet butter, cut into small pieces

Preheat oven to 350 degrees. In a medium bowl, combine the sliced peaches with sugars, cinnamon, nutmeg, flour, and butter. Toss peaches, making certain to thoroughly coat the fruit slices. Set pie filling aside and begin making the pie crust.

Pie Crusts

This recipe will make two 9-inch pie crusts.

> 2 cups all-purpose flour
> 1 tsp. salt
> 1 tsp. sugar
> ¾ cup shortening
> 6 tbsp. ice water
> 1 egg white, slightly beaten
> 1 egg, lightly beaten
> 2 tbsp. heavy cream

In a bowl, mix flour, salt, and sugar. Using a pastry blender or a fork, add shortening until flour forms small chunks. Sprinkle water into the mixture one tablespoon at a time. Toss mixture lightly with a fork until dough forms a ball. Different brands of flour may require more water to form ball.

Divide dough into two equal parts and form two separate balls. Wrap each dough ball in clean cellophane wrap. Allow dough to rest in refrigerator for approximately 20 minutes.

Lightly flour rolling surface and rolling pin. Roll one dough ball into a circle. Trim circle 1 inch larger than upside-down pie pan. Loosen dough carefully and place dough into pie pan. Trim edge even with pan. Crust is now ready for pie filling. Pour peach pie filling into pan.

Roll the second dough ball into a circle. Using another pie pan as a guide, cut the dough into a circle. The circle should extend slightly beyond the diameter of the pie pan's rim.

Moisten the edges of the pie shell that contains the peach filling with a pastry brush dipped in the beaten egg white.

Cut the top crust into 6 wedges. Position the wedges so that they slightly overlap each other over the top of the filling and crust in the pan. Press the edges of the top and bottom crusts together. Cut off any excess dough.

Combine heavy cream and beaten egg to create egg wash. Brush the top crust with the egg wash, then sprinkle with sugar. Bake in oven for 40 to 50 minutes. Makes 6 servings.

Red Velvet Cake

There is something special about a red velvet cake. The contrast between the red cake and the vanilla cream frosting is definitely eye catching when displayed in the dessert case. Although I bake and display several desserts, the red velvet cake stops customers in their tracks. Even customers who have never tasted this cake are usually very eager to purchase at least a slice.

I always find it helpful to use wax paper as a lining for the bottom of cake pans. When I am baking in the restaurant, I am usually baking several cakes at one time. I always take a few extra minutes ahead of time to cut wax paper circles the diameter of the cake pans. I use these liners along with baking release spray to ensure that I do not leave pieces of cake in the pan.

2¼ cup cake flour
2 tsp. cocoa powder
1 tsp. baking powder
1 tsp. baking soda
1 tsp. salt
1 cup vegetable oil
1½ cup sugar
1 cup buttermilk
1½ tsp. white vinegar
1 tsp. vanilla extract
¼ cup red food coloring
2 large eggs
Baking release spray

Preheat oven to 325 degrees. In a medium bowl, sift together the flour, cocoa powder, baking powder, baking soda, and salt. Set aside.

Using an electric mixer on medium speed, whisk the vegetable oil and sugar together for 4 minutes. Stop the mixer and scrape the batter from the sides of the mixing bowl.

In a pitcher combine the buttermilk, vinegar, vanilla, and food coloring. Set aside.

Turn the mixer on low speed and add one egg at a time to the oil and sugar mixture. Alternate adding the flour mixture and the buttermilk mixture until all ingredients are combined. Turn mixer to medium speed and continue mixing batter for 6 minutes or until batter is smooth.

Spray two 9-inch cake pans with baking release spray and cut out rounds of wax paper to fit the bottom of cake pans. Pour batter into two pans, dividing batter equally.

Bake on middle rack for 20 to 25 minutes until cakes are done or when a toothpick comes out clean when inserted into center of cakes. Cool cakes for 20 minutes before removing from cake pans. Prepare cream cheese icing while cake is baking. Makes 8 servings.

Cream Cheese Icing

¼ lb. cream cheese, room temperature
2 tbsp. unsalted butter, room temperature
3 cups powdered sugar
½ tsp. vanilla extract
2 tsp. pecans

In an electric mixer on low speed, whisk together the cream cheese, butter, and powdered sugar for approximately 8 minutes. Stop mixer and scrape icing from sides of bowl. Add vanilla extract and turn mixer to medium speed. Whisk for an additional 5 minutes. Spread icing on cake. Randomly place pecans on top of cake after icing. Makes 8 servings.

Index

Almost Sam's Pound Cake, 142
Appetizers, 17
Apple and Walnut Salad, 39
Apple Sauce, 33

Baked Barbecue Tuna Steak, 60
Baked Chicken with Herb Vinaigrette Dressing, 80
Baked Ham, 91
Baked Macaroni and Cheese, 106
Baked Peach Rum Chicken, 81
Baked Salmon Fillet, 49
Baked Salmon Steak, 51
Baked Stuffed Salmon with Crabmeat Stuffing, 50
Baked Tilapia Topped with Peppers and Onions, 59
Banana Nut Bread, 131
Barbecue Baby Back Ribs, 94
Barbecue Shrimp, 19
Blackened Catfish Fillet, 54
Blackened Salmon, 53
Black-Eyed-Pea Relish, 128
Black-Eyed-Pea Salad with Vinaigrette Dressing, 40
Blue Cheese Dip, 34
Braised Kale, 113
Breads and Biscuits, 129
Brown Sauce, 121
Buttermilk Biscuits, 132

Cajun Fried Shrimp, 61
Candied Sweet Potatoes, 117
Carrot Salad, 42
Cheese Grits, 105
Cheesecake, 144
Chicken and Dumplings, 82
Chicken Sauce, 122
Chicken Vegetable Soup, 37
Chocolate Cake, 148
Chocolate Cheesecake, 145
Chocolate Frosting, 149
Chocolate Pecan Pie, 147
Cocktail Meatballs, 21
Cocktail Sauce, 20
Coleslaw, 42
Collard Greens and Turnip Greens with Smoked Ham Hocks and Smoked Neck Bones, 104
Collard Greens with Smoked Turkey Wings, 103
Coq Au Vin, 86
Corn and Smoked Oyster Fritters, 22
Crab and Fresh Corn Cakes, 23
Crab Cakes with Mango Salsa, 24
Crab Cakes with Sliced Okra, 69
Crabmeat Dumplings, 68
Cranberry and Pear Relish, 31
Cream Cheese Icing, 155
Creamy Coleslaw, 43
Creamy Macaroni and Cheese, 107
Crusty Skillet Corn Bread, 134
Curry Shrimp, 62

INDEX

Deep Fried Cajun Oysters, 32
Deep-Fried Red Snapper Topped with Stewed Tomatoes and Baby Clams, 71
Desserts, 139
Dirty Rice, 109

Fish and Seafood, 47
For the Crabmeat Stuffing, 50
For the Dumplings, 83
For the Herb Mayonnaise, 52
For the Oatmeal Pancakes, 84
For the Pecan Syrup, 85
For the Spicy Mayonnaise, 89
Fresh Green Beans with Smoked Neck Bones, 113
Fried Catfish, 54
Fried Chicken, 87
Fried Dill Pickles, 111
Fried Green Tomatoes, 112
Fried Okra with Lemon Caper Sauce, 28
Fried Pecan Chicken Fingers, 29

Georgia Peach Salad, 44
Grilled Black-Eyed-Pea Patties, 25
Grilled Boneless Pork Chops, 96
Grilled Catfish, 55
Grilled Marinated Lamb Chops, 91
Grits, 105

Honey Mustard Sauce, 122
Hush Puppies, 26

Jalapeno Hush Puppies with Crabmeat, 27

Kale Pasta Primavera, 114

Lemon Caper Sauce, 28
Lemon-Marinated Filet Mignon, 90
Lobster Stuffed with Mashed Potatoes, 74

Mango Salsa, 24
Marinated Chicken Wings, 89
Meat Loaf, 92
Miniature Orange Corn Muffins with Cranberry and Pear Relish, 30
Mustard Sauce, 123

Oatmeal Pancakes Stuffed with Chicken Strips, Topped with Pecan Syrup, 84
Oxtail Ragout, 93

Pan-Grilled Beer-Marinated Pork Chops, 95
Peach Cobbler, 150
Peach Pie, 152
Peanut Butter Cheesecake with Peanut Butter Cookie Crust, 146
Pear and Apple Salsa, 126
Pecan Catfish, 55
Pesto Sauce, 124
Pie Crusts, 153
Poached Fillet of Salmon, 52
Potato-Crusted Catfish, 56
Potato Pancakes with Apple Sauce, 33
Potato Salad, 45
Poultry, Meats, and Game, 77

Rabbit and Shrimp Jambalaya, 98

INDEX

Red Velvet Cake, 154
Roasted Beets, Goat Cheese, and Red Onion Salad, 41
Roasted Potato Duet, 114
Sauces, Salsas, Relishes, and Dressings, 119

Sautéed Bananas, 143
Seafood Gumbo, 64
Seasoned Boiled Shrimp with Cocktail Sauce, 20
Shrimp and Chicken Etoufee, 67
Side Dishes, 101
Smothered Pork Chops, 96
Smothered Shrimp and Scallops, 66
Soups and Salads, 35
Southern Fried Chicken, 88
Southern Fried Whiting, 70
Spice Mixture for Blackened Fish, 53
Spicy Whole Red Snapper, 72
Spicy Wings with Blue Cheese Dip, 34
Split Pea Soup, 38
Stewed Catfish, 57
Stewed Tomatoes, 116

Strawberry Sauce, 125
Stuffed Catfish, 58
Stuffed Yellow Squash, 115
Sweet Potato and Apple Casserole, 118
Sweet Potato Bread, 135
Sweet Potato Pancakes with Pecans, 136

Tartar Sauce, 125
Three Cheese Baked Macaroni and Cheese, 108
Tomato, Onion, and Basil Salad, 45
Truffle Vinaigrette Dressing, 41

Vegetable Soup, 39
Vinaigrette Dressing, 40

Watermelon Salsa, 127
White Rice, 110
Whole Baked Red Snapper Stuffed with Spinach, 73

Yellow Squash Casserole, 117
Yogurt Sauce, 126

Index